Father Bill —
Are you sure you don't want your wonderful class to tag along? We are such fun — And besides, who will you pick about me or Bob, who will you pick. Enjoyed it!
Deidre

"Australia's Great Barrier Reef is
unquestionably one of the remaining
natural wonders of the world
and is without equal as a marine treasure."

Howard
Thanks again —
As opposed to
Reef Diving
Good luck
Tropical women.
Bring back some
Health!

Hey Bob's,
Ring the Rebel
That from # Deidre
to make you read upside down.
Thanks for the great times
Blake, Kinda dude,
Francisca
Dad

Bill,
You lucky guy!
NICE long summer you have
this year. HAVE FUN, Live
Long & Prosper & all that
stuff & thanks for the
class. It was A BLAST!
Mily

Bill,
Thanks for a great 10 weeks!
we couldn't have picked a
nicer guy!
Sheryl

Bill,
thanks for a great time and
taking the hassle we gave you.
Have fun in Australia and I
hope to see you soon.
Bob

The
Great
Barrier
Reef

A Guide to the Islands & Resorts

by Arne and Ruth Werchick

Wide World Publishing/Tetra

Wide World Publishing/Tetra
P.O. Box 476
San Carlos, CA 94070

SECOND EDITION—Revised and Updated

Printed in the United States of America.

Library of Congress Cataloging-in-Publication Data

Werchick, Arne.
    The Great Barrier Reef.

    Includes index.
    1. Great Barrier Reef (Qld.)—Description and trave—Guide-books.
I. Werchick, Ruth. II. Title.
DU280. G68W47   1988   919.43'0463   87-51278
ISBN 0-933174-55-1

CONTENTS

Islands of the Great Barrier Reef and their Resorts

Coastal Cities & Towns 195

Coastal Cities & Towns

More Interesting Things 217

sailing the Great Barrier Reef

Introduction

In 1984 the Australian Tourist Commission, Qantas Airlines and the Queensland government among others intensified dramatically the campaign to bring more visitors to Australia. In the first three months of TV commercials in the U.S., over 100,000 Americans sought further information about travel "down under". In 1984 during its first four months as an international jet gateway, Cairns on Australia's northeast coast and adjacent to the Great Barrier Reef was the point of entry for almost 9,000 American visitors. Since then Qantas has been bringing a steady stream of Americans through this expanding gateway city, and the success of the hit movie Crocodile Dundee has focused even more attention on the tropical north.

We had visited Australia before and knew we would return to see more of the Barrier Reef. Perhaps it was the advertising or just our happy memories of a comfortably superb and exciting vacation — for visiting Australia is like visiting with cousins with whom we have much in common but who live in a place in so many respects quite different than ours; in any event we just had to explore the Great Barrier Reef more fully.

Our plans first took us to a book store, then another, then the largest in the City, then to the Library of Congress index. We were astounded, but there was no travel book which described the resort islands of the Great Barrier Reef in any detail, and precious little in print in the United States about the Reef at all. As we gathered travel brochures and government promotional literature from Australia, Queensland, the Whitsunday area, and other sources, we found that Australians themselves were unclear about many features of travel to North Queensland.

Sailing the Great Barrier Reef

Depending upon whom we relied, for example, we found that Lindeman Island, a resort island in the Whitsunday Passage, was either 67 or 70 or 72 or 75 kilometers off the coast from Mackay. Not that the actual distance was that important, so long as the pilots with Lindeman Aerial Services and the captains of the giant catamaran ferries always hit the island right on the mark. But we were intrigued that descriptions of accommodations, prices, amenities and the like differed so.

Thus was born the idea for this book. It was a first effort at travel writing for us, but as much a labor of affection for one of the truly magic places in the world as a desire to try to fill a gap in travel information for the increasing thousands who will respond to the lure of this incredible marine holiday just as we have done. Since publication not that long ago, many new developments on the Barrier Reef and return trips have lead to this updating. We are also deeply indebted to many nice people who, having read the book and visited our favorite places, were kind enough to offer suggestions to be included in this expanded and revised edition.

Arne & Ruth Werchick
Sausalito, California

Darwin

Coral Sea

Northern
Territory

GREAT BARRIER REEF

Queensland

Western
Australia

South
Australia

Brisbane

New South
Wales

Perth

Sydney

Adelaide

Victoria
Melbourne

Tasmania

AUSTRALIA

The Great Barrier Reef
•Coral

Australia's Great Barrier Reef is unquestionably one of the remaining natural wonders of the world and is without equal as a marine treasure. To see it and particularly to walk upon it at low tide gives a person an incredibly vivid sense of the power of the ocean and of the billions of coral polyps which over the ages   make up a reef miles wide in places. To explore the islands, atolls and fringing reefs which owe their birth and continued existence to the protection of the great Outer Reef with the ocean crashing against its sheer wall on the one side and with placid pools and lagoons inside this immense natural enclosure imposes a sense of the vastness of the sea and its marine life and a deep appreciation of the beauty of some of the oldest and the most varied forms of life on earth.

This huge living coral structure, occupying more than 72,000 square miles of ocean, extends from New Guinea in the Coral Sea southward to the Pacific Ocean below the fabled Tropic of Capricorn, which at 23º27' latitude south of the equator marks the southern edge of the Torrid Zone. Some two thousand subordinate reefs — some developing over the past 15,000 years — are interspersed and often interlocked to make this continental barrier, having grown as the sea level on the northeast continental shelf of Australia rose perhaps 150' over thousands of years to its present level, covering sites suitable for coral settlement and growth.

Glancing at a world map gives an idea of the tropical   significance of this location. Rio de Janeiro lies near the Tropic of Capricorn. The northern equivalent of these latitudes — the tropic of Cancer at 23º27' latitude north — incorporates Hawaii and the tropical Caribbean islands. These are the sunniest latitudes on earth.

The Outer Barrier Reef follows the coast of Queensland, Australia's huge northeastern state, for 1258 miles. (Imagine a wall extending from the west coast of the United States roughly half way to Hawaii.) The

Australian Tourist Commission's very useful publication, *Destination Australia* , tells us it runs

> *from the very tip of Cape York Peninsula in the North of Queensland to below Gladstone in the south. Located 12 to 31 miles (20 to 50 km) offshore, the Reef acts as a barrier against the Pacific Ocean. The Outer Barrier Reef, an extensive coral platform, rises from the ocean floor; some sections are awash, others just beneath the waves. At low tide, parts of the coral mass are bared and you can explore the great coral grounds.*

The English explorer Captain James Cook aboard the *Endeavor* in 1770 was the first European to discover this incredible reef — at least the first to live to describe the voyage. The next European to pass through the region was Captain Bligh in an open boat after the mutiny on the *Bounty* en route from Tahiti to Timor in the Indian Ocean in May of 1789. Since its discovery by Europeans, first navigators and later scientists have puzzled over its origins and its immensity. Much is still unknown about this thousand mile wall running half the length of a continent just beneath the surface of the ocean, such that just within the past year a new deep water channel through the reef was discovered, cutting as much as a half day for freighters carrying commerce between Japan and Australia.

To the north of Cairns along the Cape York Peninsula, the Outer Reef is succession of solid barrier ribbon reefs with tortuous passages, some of them 50 miles long. Inside this continental shelf are numerous subordinate reefs. As you move to the southern extremes, the Reef is much less continuous, more a succession of massive segments of platform reef — many several miles long and wide — with navigable channels. The lagoon filling the thousands of square miles between the Outer Reef and the mainland is literally a cornucopia of smaller coral reefs, coral cays and atolls and, near the coast, with hundreds of continental and bush islands which the ages have gradually pulled from the mainland itself and eons later provided with their own fringing reefs.

You can explore on foot (at low tide) and by snorkel and scuba diving many parts of the Great Barrier Reef itself and many   of the abundant fringing reefs which have grown around the sheltered islands, and you will marvel at the variety of life ordinarily hidden beneath the sea. Almost all of the resorts in North Queensland offer excursions of one sort or another to the Outer Reef. These may be by boat or by air, and some resorts actually have barges moored permanently at the Outer Reef itself.

The Great Barrier Reef never contacts the mainland, and to see and appreciate it one must visit the varied and beautiful islands of the area. To do so not only offers the excitement of the Reef itself but also promises one of the best tropical island vacations possible in the world — offering an exciting array of unique vacation resorts, many set amidst national parks or naturally beautiful unspoiled surroundings, but each different than the other and almost all with but one resort to an island.

The higher islands off the Queensland coast are generally situated closer to the mainland. Most rise abruptly. Many of the islands within the protected waters of the Outer Reef are bordered by "fringing coral reefs" within which thrive marine environments which are miniature versions of those within the Outer Reef itself. These subordinate reefs develop in shallower water rather close to the coasts of the high islands. They tend to be U-shaped because of the currents and winds. Depending upon the degree of protection, the weather conditions and other factors, some of these inner reefs are richer in coral and marine life than many portions of the Outer Reef itself and offer fantastic surface and underwater sightseeing opportunities.

In all the Great Barrier Reef embraces nineteen developed islands with resort facilities, 2500 named reefs, 250 named continental islands, 71 named coral cays, and a total of more than 600 islands. All of the resort islands are leaseholds of government property except Bedarra and Dunk which became freeholds through legislative anomaly early this century. Magnetic Island, not really a resort island in the true sense but rather a suburban island with many motel and lodging facilities, is a considerably larger freehold island, parts of which later became converted to hotels and resorts. Most of the resort islands have also been classified in whole or in part as Australian national parks.

Many of these islands started with government approval as sheep stations or cattle ranches or other small business ventures and were later converted to resort facilities because, by quirk of Australian law, the leases were transferable. Yet today, because there were no early pastoral or other business leases on them, the large majority of Barrier Reef islands remain entirely and beautifully vacant.

The Australian Great Barrier Reef Marine Park Act of 1975 establishes a region of over 17,000 square miles as protected area with plans ultimately to add the majority of the Barrier Reef to this Marine Park. [For information about the Park, you can write to the Great Barrier Reef

Marine Park Authority, P.O. Box 1379, Townsville, Qld. 4810, Australia.]
In recognition of the unique significance of this natural treasure, the
United Nations Education, Scientific and Cultural Organization in
October 1981 added the Great Barrier Reef to the World Heritage List.

Coral

Coral reefs are built over hundreds and thousands of years by microscopic
living coral polyps, minute relatives of jellyfish and sea anemones. These
remarkable tiny engineers ingest sea water, filter out nourishment, and
from this "manufacture" calcium carbonate, which we know as simple
limestone, which becomes their external skeleton of hard coral. When
not feeding the polyps usually withdraw into their skeletons which
appear as cylindrical containers, called corallites. Different types of coral
feed at different times of day, and while snorkeling or diving you can
recognize feeding coral by the fact that it appears distinctly softer   and
fuzzier all over, while those polyps that are not feeding will appear to be
smoother and harder.

Generation after coral generation is born, lives and dies   atop one
another. As they die, their infinitesimal "bones" interlock and pile one
on another to add to the bulk of a particular reef, and a new generation of
colorful living coral replaces its ancestors. Coralline algae and other
microscopic denizens of the ocean add to the structure and provide the
organic cement which binds the reef together so firmly that after a point it
becomes as hard as solid ground.

Coral reefs themselves become centers of sea life. Plants grow on and
around them. Small and large sea creatures use them as sources of food,
shelter from the sun, protection from predators. They wax and wane over
the decades as the conditions of the sea change and as predatory forces
attack or ignore them.

There are hundreds of different coral species. Dozens of species of soft
corals do not have limestone skeletons and look like marine vegetation.
The four hundred species of hard corals fall broadly into two main
categories: branching, such as staghorn, needle, and knobby corals along
with the beautiful ephemeral coral fans; or rounded like boulders, some
of the most dramatic of which are the brain corals (almost perfectly round
structures, from under six inches to huge "bommies " twenty-five or

more feet in diameter, which actually appear to have convolutions like the human brain) or large single-polyp mushroom coral (so called because it looks like the bottom side of a mushroom), also sometimes called razor coral because of the hundreds of individual razor-thin septa which radiate from its central mouth.

Coral needs favorable conditions to survive and thrive. Until very recently, it was believed that water had to be shallow enough for abundant sunlight to penetrate to support coral polyps which need plant life for oxygen and nutrition. Recent scientific research has uncovered algae which exist at depths previously thought impossible, living on the tiny fraction of sunlight which reaches the sea floor at eight hundred feet. Water does have to be quite salty, clear and warm (with average ocean temperatures above 64 even in colder months). Most living reefs are less than 100 feet deep, although existence of reefs to depths more than 1/4 mile has been recognized, and this remains a scientific puzzle leading scholars to evolve theories of changing ocean depths over the centuries.

Coral reefs will not develop when they encounter fresh water, and thus even the Great Barrier Reef itself comes to an abrupt end off New Guinea where it encounters the muddy river waters flowing from the mountains of Papua. The cuts and channels which interrupt reefs, and the major sea channels which have been discovered to allow navigation across the Barrier Reef itself, mirror the variations in the flow and quality of the sea, sometimes reflecting river entrances on the adjacent coastline. Even the most perfect island reef must have at least one break to permit the lagoon to fill and empty with fresh sea water lest the entire inner fringing reef die.

Coral dies when exposed to the sun for more than a few hours. While it produces heavy mucous secretions to protect itself from low tides and for brief exposure to the sun, prolonged exposure is fatal. Thus if removed from the nurturing sea for any length of time, areas of dead coral are left behind.

Living coral exists in a broad array of colors, but closer to the surface it seems to favor yellows, browns, greens and blues. Reds are less plentiful, and blacks are found generally at much greater depths. When coral dies it turns white or pale grey or dirty beige with the exception of the deep water black coral and only a few of the red corals. All coral dies when removed from the sea. (The samples you occasionally see for sale at souvenir stands have usually been recolored using food dyes.) There is therefore no point to consider breaking the rules of the Barrier Reef by snapping off pieces of coral for a colorful souvenir. Aside from the fact that you will end up with a relatively nondescript piece of plain white coral, the powerfully unpleasant smell of the decaying polyps could be substantial punishment for your misdeed.

The Barrier Reef and its inner lagoons and fringing reefs is not the place for collecting corals and shells. There are numerous other island nations in the Pacific which have an abundance of marine life and do not currently object — vigorously, at any rate — to the taking of sea creatures as souvenirs. Australia, however, has good reason to want to protect the treasure of the Barrier Reef, and you will be reminded at each resort of the importance of leaving the Reef intact. Australian visitors, we might add, respect this request and are almost unanimously careful about the health of their Reef.

As living coral reefs grow and grow over decades and centuries, they collect other marine debris as well, including sand and pieces of seaborne broken coral.   This leads to the formation of coral cays (generally pronounced "keys") which gradually develop   at the end of the reef away from the prevailing wind because of the action of wind, sun and sea. As this new "land" forms, the ocean and the wind, and perhaps bird life from nearby land, will later bring living seeds, leading to the development of the tropical vegetation commonly found on coral islands. If you fly over the waters inside the main reef, particularly toward the northern end, you will see many of these developing reef islands of the distant future.

These cays are quite distinct from the islands usually found closer to the coast — the continental and bush islands — which are formed either by ancient volcanic activity or by having broken off from the coastline to which they were attached.   Cays are commonly found immediately adjacent to the inner reefs and on the Outer Reef itself, but almost invariably at quite some distance from the mainland.

Coral reefs support an incredible array of marine flora and fauna. Here you may find sponges, shells, giant clams, sea   cucumber (beche de mer, a delicacy in some oriental societies), an incredible array of shell creatures, benign starfish and the hideous and destructive Crown of Thorns starfish. If you look closely you can see six different species of giant sea turtles: green, leatherback, flatback, loggerhead, hawksbill and Pacific Ridley, all protected by law. Even in shallower waters you will see more varieties of vividly colored tropical fish than you believed existed anywhere, ranging in size from a couple of inches to well over a foot. To treat the eye you will see good sized angels, surgeon fish, parrot fish, damsel fish, trumpets, clown fish and every other small tropical imaginable. You will also see or fish for sweetlip, emperors, snapper or coral trout which may exceed two or even three feet in length. In deeper waters the Barrier Reef supports the largest marlin in the world, along with shark, sailfish, tuna and other exciting deep sea sport fish. In all there have been 1500 species of fish identified in the Great Barrier Reef region.

Coral provides hours of fascination and delight. Unfortunately it also has a serious predator along the Great Barrier Reef. In the late 1960s scientists discovered that the population of a formerly obscure creature, the Crown of Thorns, a spiny dozen-legged starfish, had suddenly and inexplicably increased dramatically. This rather ugly echinoderm, which can grow to over a foot in diameter, feeds on living coral tissue leaving a trail of bleached white dead coral in its wake.

When the Crown of Thorns is less numerous, with just a few per acre, they feed at night digesting perhaps fifty square feet of coral a year — a limited assault which a healthy coral reef can usually tolerate. When their numbers reach the thousands on a segment of reef, however, these predatory starfish make short work of the reef, producing ninety percent destruction and leaving broad patches of permanently devastated reef. These predators, which may live for years, breed in midsummer when the female releases millions of eggs into the water. Fortunately the mortality rate for this spawn is very high, but the potential for epidemic spread is always present.

For reasons still not clearly understood the infestation of the '60s and '70s, which some doomsayers feared would devastate the entire length of the Great Barrier Reef before a solution could be found, retreated as mysteriously as it had begun. Is the danger passed? Although we saw some Crown of Thorns, and many charter trip operators — particularly in the north — conduct periodic forays on their days off to keep the population of predators in their area of the Reef under control, the government seems satisfied that the peril is history. Recently, however, The *Bulletin*, Australia's weekly news magazine affiliated with *Newsweek*, featured a cover story proclaiming that the plague has returned. Although there seems to be little agreement with this frightening prophecy, the Great Barrier Reef does remain vulnerable to this danger of devastation until scientists understand better what produces this massive invasion and how to deter it.

Hayman Island

Seeing and Doing
•snorkeling
•scuba diving
•more to see and do
•safety & health

Island holidays obviously conjure visions of sandy beaches, swimming in the ocean and in elegant   resort pools — perhaps with the tropical bar beside or in the middle for a bit of cool refreshment. Then there is plenty of rest and relaxation, and maybe golf or tennis, and of course a good restaurant here and there for relaxed dinners followed, perhaps, with some music and a nice bar for a nightcap. The Great Barrier Reef of course provides ample doses of classic island vacation, usually in the least crowded island resorts imaginable, but it offers many experiences that few other areas of the world can match.

Snorkeling

Whether or not you have ever been much for water sports, or even if you are not a terribly strong swimmer, you will never forgive yourself for visiting the Barrier Reef without skin diving, or snorkeling, in these intensely blue translucent waters where underwater visibility fifteen or even twenty-five feet is not unusual. Snorkeling is named for its chief piece of equipment, the snorkel, which is nothing more than a rubberized tube with a mouthpiece which you insert in your mouth while floating or swimming on the surface of the water.

This twelve to eighteen inch long tube is curved upward behind your head, so while you are staring with fascination at the coral and fish beneath you through a tempered glass face mask, you are also breathing comfortably through the tube from the air above you. Your bathing costume is complete with the addition of a pair of swim fins which give you tremendous leg power in the water; even if you could never tread water in a swimming pool, diving fins virtually allow you to stand upright in the ocean with your arms out of water or to move forward swiftly with relaxed leg action.

Believe us: snorkeling is very, very easy. You don't have to dive into water with crashing waves or perform feats of strength or daring in the water to be good at this simple sport. At each resort, skilled and very cautious boat operators will take you out to quiet waters, show you how to snorkel, and then watch you like a hawk to make sure you don't get into any difficulty. Lots of snorkeling is in waters shallow enough to stand upright in, but do be careful not to stand on delicate coral and perhaps damage it permanently. The best snorkeling is also in calmer seas. Face it, fish aren't entirely stupid; they prefer calm waters too. Fragile coral doesn't do particularly well in turbulent seas either. In many instances — at Heron Island or Hayman Island, for example, you can enjoy the sport by walking into the sea right off the beach at the edge of the resort and yet see thousands of beautiful fish and dozens of corals in shallow calm waters.

If we still haven't soothed your deepest fears, you can go to a dive shop in your home town and take a brief snorkel lesson in their swimming pool. In fact such a stop, with or without the instructions, will be a wise idea. Although all of the resorts will lend or rent snorkel gear to you, one problem which you do encounter with snorkeling is finding equipment among the resort's supply which will fit you precisely.

When you get to the point where you love snorkeling so much that they have to drag you out of the water with a hook (which point we predict you will reach on your second day watching the fish), you want swim fins and particularly a face mask which fit as perfectly as possible. You may also want a mask which matches your vision correction if you wear glasses or contact lenses. (We both wear contacts; one of us snorkels with lenses, while the other prefers the prescription face mask, so take your choice.) Your dive shop can probably outfit you with a face mask fitted with a lens that is a very close approximation of most corrections for simple near- or far-sightedness for under $100 including the cost of the face mask. Quality face masks with clear tempered glass will cost anywhere from $40 to over $100. You need not bring snorkel gear to Australia; resorts and boat operators make it available to their guests. By carrying your snorkel gear — particularly a comfortable mask — with you, however, you avoid the risk that the particular resort is out of your size or simply cannot give you a mask which keeps the water out of your eyes.

If you're still a little nervous about languidly swimming around a boat in water which might be deeper than you are tall, buy and bring one of the new light-weight belts which add a bit of support in the water. Even if you're very, very nervous about going in the water, do not give up hope;

look into buying the least expensive available type of what divers call a *buoyancy compensator* or *BC*. This is nothing other than one of those inflatable life vests you have seen flight attendants on airlines demonstrate at the beginning of over-water flights. It is a standard scuba gear to permit the divers to adjust buoyancy because of the weight of tanks and other gear they carry, but it can be a useful tool for a new snorkeler. It fits over your head and straps around your waist. You blow as much air into it as you need to support yourself comfortably on the water's surface and could theoretically float on calm seas until the Coast Guard arrives. It is the ultimate tranquilizer for the nervous snorkeler, but we predict that by the end of your first week you will wonder why you spent $75 for a BC. Oh well, you can always give it to your kids or to your favorite airline.

To find the best snorkeling in a particular area, look to where the coral thrives. There is little marine life of interest   in areas where the reef has died. This means not too much prolonged exposure to direct sun at low tide and not too much crashing surf. Generally the best time for snorkeling is just after low tide on the incoming sea because the fish do not need to seek the protection of deeper water and shady crannies to escape the direct sun or low tide. The resort staff will gladly tell you how to find the best snorkeling.

Do remember that your back is exposed to the sun as you absent-mindedly drift with the current almost hypnotized by the teeming life just beneath the surface. A tee shirt or strong sun block or both should be part of the equipment of every snorkeler.

the joy of snorkeling

Scuba Diving

Many diving afficionados claim that the Great Barrier Reef offers some of the best natural conditions for scuba diving in the entire world. There are few wrecks for exploration, but virtually everything else is there — plant and animal life, walls, caves, crevices, deep coral formations, great photographic opportunities — all in an environment as safe for divers as anywhere in the world.

Several islands offer diving opportunities, and each resort claims to be the best. Heron, Lizard and Hamilton Islands perhaps now advertise diving more than the others, but nine other islands (Daydream, Great Keppel, Green, Fitzroy, Hayman, Hinchinbrook, Long, Lady Elliot and South Molle) also offer at least some scuba diving opportunities. A few offer diving instruction packages. Tank refills are available at Daydream, Green, Hayman, Heron, Lady Elliot, Lizard, South Molle, and from the independent dive shop on Great Keppel, as well as at dive facilities in the major coastal towns. Most islands, however, currently do not have much in the way of rental equipment, and only a few offer specialized boating services for the serious deep water diver. Most all islands do offer charter services to specially good tank dive spots in waters   in the vicinity of the particular resort or to the Outer Reef. Hayman Island, for example, offers trips which will take divers to some highly regarded spots off the island and near adjacent Hook Island which offer excellent dive opportunities. Lizard Island has several outstanding dive spots within an hour boat ride of the resort, as do Hamilton and Heron.

All resorts and charter boat operators indicate that they will definitely require that you have a regular valid diving certificate from one of the internationally recognized dive organizations such as PADI or NAUI or enroll in their diving program before they will furnish diving gear and services, and in addition some may expect you to bring your diving log. All of the resorts have masks and fins available for guests for use in snorkeling (but a few do charge rental fees). If you are at all particular, however, you will want to bring your own. Regulators are rather scarce (with the exception of bigger towns and Hamilton Island), so you definitely should think about bringing your own. Wet suits and buoyancy compensators can be rented on several but not all islands; if you are travelling to different resorts and uninhabited islands, you will want to bring your own or call beforehand to check on availability. Tanks and weight belts are generally available.

More to see and do

All of the resorts make available a wide variety of equipment for enjoying the water. At many islands, the use of this gear is included in your daily room rate, while at others varying charges are exacted for different activities. All of the resorts offer small sailing catamarans of the 11' to 14' variety and will happily show you how to enjoy them safely and comfortably in the bay right in front of the resort. There are pedal boats and even huge tricycles that two people can sit on and pedal across the sea on top of the water. Windsurfers and paddle boards are everywhere. Most resorts also have small motor dinghies which you can take out for trips to nearby beaches; most charge for fuel, but Bedarra, Orpheus and Lizard make no extra charge for the motor boats.

Among other water sports found at Great Barrier Reef resorts, you will be offered paraflying, water skiing, trips in glass bottom boats, picnic excursions to adjacent islands, trips to underwater observatories and of course day and half-day fishing expeditions. Or there are small boats and jetties from which you may just drop in a line and pull out a meal. All of the kitchens will be happy to prepare your catch for your dinner.

Most of the resorts have fresh water swimming pools for your lounging and cooling off pleasure. At some, water volley ball is a popular sport. At others reading and enjoying a tropical drink are the busiest pool activities.

When you have absorbed enough water activity for the day, you will find fascinating bush walking trails on most islands where you can see some of the most unusual bird and animal life outside of a zoo. On a few islands to the north, there are also rain forests which provide an exciting and perfectly safe walk through a tropical jungle.

Most resorts offer tennis courts (of widely varying quality) and a few have golf courses. Some have added archery ranges.

This is a new generation of island resorts on a group of uncrowded, generally unspoiled islands. There was little if any indigenous population on most of these islands for centuries, and there are only a couple of islands with any permanent residents aside from resort staff and the personnel attached to lighthouses or research stations. The resort islands are almost all surrounded by nearby totally uninhabited islands for you to visit and explore for the day, often entirely by yourselves while the resort staff leaves you quietly alone and will return for you at whatever hour you specify. Except on Hamilton and Magnetic Islands, the only vehicles here are support and transport machines for the resorts. There are few roads and, when away from your hotel, no noises except the sea and the birds. There are few places in the world combining the opportunity for a vacation both loaded with in activity yet rich in solitude and quiet.

Safety and Health

Australia is very health and safety conscious. Food and water are extremely safe and pure. Airlines are at least as tightly regulated for safety as in the United States if not more so. The captains who skipper your boats for island tours are specially licensed, and those who can sail you out to the Outer Barrier Reef itself are experienced and specially licensed with what are called "50 mile/50 ton" certificates.

Walking on the Reef is not possible at all times. Australians are very safety conscious about such things and closely observe tide and weather conditions. To be sure that you will be able actually to walk on the Great Barrier Reef, you must allow time for tides and weather to be right.

There is little danger in the Barrier Reef area from plant or animal life. There is less shark peril to swimmers or divers in the reef-protected waters off the resort islands than off the coasts of the United States. All of Australia reported only 20 attacks — one quarter of them fatalities — during the period 1970-80. Only the smallest and least menacing sharks are rarely seen inside the fringing reefs which surround most resort islands. In our own visits, we have yet to see even a baby shark during a snorkeling expedition around these islands. If you would like to see these fearsome predators in a natural setting but in complete safety, there is a fascinating collection at the magnificent new _Great Barrier Reef Wonderland_ in Townsville.

The sea bottom is relatively benign except for a few urchins and even fewer stone fish which must not be stepped upon. Probably the least expected, yet remote, danger comes from a very few shell creatures — particularly the attractive cones — which pack a very dangerous wallop if you were to pick them up and particularly to those who have put them into a pocket. When on an excursion near the Outer Reef, your skipper almost certainly will warn you against stepping on the obnoxious Crown of Thorns starfish — which eats and destroys the coral reef — and also has hundreds of stickers which could inflict a nasty sting. So long as you are inside the fringing reefs swimming and looking, you are essentially in no danger from natural life. If you want to explore the sea bottom by hand, it is important to wear gloves and to discuss the presence of any particular hazard with resort staff before venturing out. A good rule for complete safety while exploring the seabed is, when in doubt, not to pick up living creatures and not to put your fingers where you cannot see them.

The only serious maritime peril to swimmers and divers comes from the December to March invasion of venomous sea wasps,   also known as box jelly fish. These translucent creatures looking somewhat like an inverted floating plastic bag have a box-shaped head about four to six inches across and are almost invisible without polaroid glasses. They may cast a bluish shadow on a sandy bottom in full sun. Their trailing tentacles with hundreds of minute and poisonous stingers can deliver a potentially fatal jolt to a human. These dangerous creatures which breed in inland waters are responsible for more fatalities in Australia waters than sharks, crocodiles, stone fish and all other maritime creatures together. Anti-venom serum is stocked at hospitals and other facilities on tropical coasts in Australia.

Fortunately for Barrier Reef visitors these creatures drift mainly near the surface and along the coast and rarely are found near the islands or farther out toward the reef. Coastal resorts and the beach at Picnic Bay on Magnetic Island are often protected by special nets during the jellyfish season. Preferring shallow water near river outlets, the animals are only rarely seen over coral or weed beds. They therefore have not constituted a serious problem on Barrier Reef islands or in the deeper waters frequented by divers, and none of the resorts has been menaced by them.

If there are any particular local perils, we have found the resorts and boat operators in the area to be very meticulous and conscientious about warning of even minimal risks. We have listed the dangers here about which we were informed, but we encountered virtually none of them during our travels except for   seeing a few Crown of Thorns and a very occasional but quite visible black sea urchin with its long spikes clearly warning the snorkeler not to touch.

One truly serious peril about which many resorts don't really warn adequately is the sun. You are very much in the tropics here, and the sun is exceptionally intense. Without protection the average person exposed to the midday sun (between 10:00 a.m. and 2:30 p.m.) will begin to burn in just 12 minutes! After 30 minutes you will experience appreciable discomfort; after one hour, peeling and blistering; and after two hours, possible permanent damage. Clouds give virtually no additional protection from the sun; being on or near the water intensifies the risk because of reflected ultraviolet exposure. Even a suntan doesn't offer much real protection.

There are only two ways to deal with the risk of over-exposure to the sun: either stay out of the sun ("Stay out of the sun!", you're saying, "but then why the devil did I fly 7500 miles"); or be smart and exercise extreme prudence by wearing hats and cover-ups, be aware of the time and intensity of your exposure to the sun, and *use protective lotions generously and regularly* . Now that sun lotions and creams are rated by protective power relative to how long they multiply natural resistance to sunburn, the choice is easier. We recommend that you take with you and make regular use of sun blocks — that is, the newest waterproof lotions or creams rated 29' or maximum protection — or their close relatives. And if you do get a sunburn, do stay out of the midday sun for at least a day or two. Don't worry; you'll be pleasantly surprised to note that you soon build up that great tan even with this maximum degree of sun protection, and your vacation won't be interrupted by the need to spend a week indoors writing postcards telling every one how much fun you were having.

One last precaution: during certain seasons and only on some islands, small biting insects — particularly what Australians call the sand fly, which is more like a flea — can be a terrible nuisance. Locals get used to them and are often unbothered. If you are hypersensitive or easily annoyed by these obnoxious creatures, remember to use any of the modern bug repellents liberally, especially around your feet and ankles. We found that every resort sold moderately effective repellents, although we didn't see many creams or ointments designed exclusively to relieve the swelling and itching if you are attacked, so you may want to bring a tube of over-the- counter cortisone cream just in case.

Lizard Island

landing on Great Keppel

Get Ready, Get Set
•transportation
•attire
•photography
•getting ready

Transportation

There are several airlines currently serving Australia from the United States, and there are several options available to get you to the Great Barrier Reef. Airfares are quite competitive for U.S. travel to this region, so the visitor has an interesting range of choices. We should also mention that Sydney's Kingsford-Smith airport, with its separate international and domestic terminals, is efficient and an easy entry or departure point, while Cairns remains small and uncrowded.

Qantas, Australia's own international air carrier, flies non-stop to Sydney from Los Angeles and San Francisco. In addition, on alternate nights Qantas flights leave Los Angeles, San Francisco and Vancouver, stop in Honolulu for an hour or so, and then go on to Sydney (with ongoing service to Melbourne), Cairns, or Nadi, gateway airport for the island nation of Fiji. Qantas' 747s are generally full, but their outstanding congenial staff usually make the trip very pleasant. There are no additional charges for drinks and headsets on Qantas, and it is not unusual for them to hand wine drinkers a full bottle of Australian wine rather than have to keep coming around to refill your glass.

If you have set out to visit the Barrier Reef directly as   the first or only destination on your journey, Qantas' twice-a-week direct service connecting the west coast through Honolulu to Cairns, with on-going service to Brisbane and connections to Sydney and Melbourne is probably the most convenient. Using this very fine airline, it is also possible to visit other points in Australia, and Qantas does offer a circle fare allowing multiple stops on a round trip from the West Coast so long as you do not retrace your steps. You could therefore add stops in Brisbane, Sydney and Melbourne and see much of Australia for the same fare. (Since Qantas serves New Guinea from Sydney, it is also possible to add an exotic optional side trip to Papua by including the Sydney-Port Moresby-Sydney service on this ticket, since Qantas does not serve New Guinea from any other gateway and therefore permits this retracing of steps on its circle fare.)

The only major criticism of Qantas' service comes from several people who protest the lack of preassigned seats. As a result, and because Qantas rigidly assigns entire sections for smoking and non-smokers, many non-smokers have been required to undergo the discomfort of a long flight in the smoking section — and a few have vowed never to fly Qantas again until this situation is rectified. The lack of advance seat assignments also makes for rather long lines at check-in counters on flight nights. We would expect that a few letters to management ultimately should cure this deficiency in a fully computerized and otherwise extremely efficient and able airline.

One very small inconvenience which you must bear if you use the otherwise very convenient Qantas service rather than domestic carriers for internal flights between major cities in Australia is that, because it is certified exclusively as an international carrier, each stop along the way is treated as an international flight with immigration requirements. This proved no great delay   in Cairns or Brisbane, but we found ourselves in long lines at customs at Sydney's Kingsford Smith airport.

Air New Zealand offers excellent regular DC-10 service from Los Angeles to Australia via Auckland or Christchurch and   permits multiple stops en route on the same fare (with occasional "super-low round-trip" fares ex-Los Angeles). The Australia cities included on this circle route are Melbourne, Sydney and Brisbane. By flying Air New Zealand, you could also add stops in Tahiti and Fiji. Because traffic is through Auckland, the airline obviously encourages you to include a visit to New Zealand. The airline staff is particularly congenial, the planes are sparkling clean, and the amenities were just about as nice as one can find in international travel. We found their service to be particularly prompt (with flights on a couple of legs actually departing a few minutes early because all reserved passengers had checked in), efficient and pleasant, although some American travellers might want to see if Air New Zealand has changed their no-alcohol-served-on-Sunday rule before booking a Sunday flight. Qantas and UTA, the French long-distance carrier in the Pacific, also fly to Tahiti with service from Los Angeles to Papeete and on to Sydney. Continental Airline flies from the West Coast to Sydney via Honolulu as does CP Air (Canadian Airlines International) out of Vancouver. In 1985 United Air Lines bought from Pan American all of its Pacific routes, including Australia, making United a major force in Pacific area travel. United's long-term plans for Australia have not been announced, other than the fact that they have continued the service previously offered by Pan Am with Los Angeles-Sydney service.

Airline service all over the South Pacific is in the process of major changes and substantial growth, so you should work closely with a travel adviser as you prepare for your trip to see exactly what exciting combinations are available. Small regional airlines are expanding, and new international routes are being opened, particularly with the addition of new fuel-efficient jumbo jets to   southern hemisphere airline fleets. Qantas, for example, has taken over management of Fiji's Air Pacific which has routes from Honolulu to Nadi (which is pronounced "Nandi" in Fijiian and,   although not the capitol, is the international gateway to this nation of hundreds of islands), and Nadi to Brisbane, and they are looking for new airports to serve with Qantas' new Boeing 767s. Ansett, Australia's private domestic carrier, also serves Port Vila, capitol of Vanuatu, from Brisbane as well as Christchurch on the south island of New Zealand from Melbourne. Moreover, with the intense advertising campaign by both Australian and Queensland tourist commissions, it seems inevitable that more international air carriers will add direct routes from the U.S. west coast to Cairns, Townsville and Brisbane which are all vying for increased international air traffic.

Whether your holiday involves combining visits to several nations of the South Pacific, or a visit to all or just a part of Australia, the key to reaching the Barrier Reef by air will be getting to one of the gateway cities of Queensland: Cairns, Townsville, Prosperpine, Mackay, Rockhampton, Gladstone, Bundaberg or Brisbane. From there the resort islands are reached by light   aircraft connection or boat. With few exceptions, these resorts   do not interconnect with each other by regular air, ferry or launch service, so visiting more than one resort will most often require going back to the coast.

Travel between major cities of Australia is via one of its two jet carriers, privately owned Ansett or government owned Australian Airlines, formerly called TransAustralia Airlines or TAA. There is a non-competition compact between these two carriers—not due to expire until 1990 — that they will operate the same routes at virtually the same times. This means that while Australian   Airlines offered daily

Sydney-Townsville service at 7:55 a.m., noon and 4:00 p.m., Ansett offered the same connection at 7:55 a.m., 11:50 a.m., and 4:15 p.m. Just about the only major exception to this dual service is that currently Ansett is the exclusive jet air carrier to the resort on Hamilton Island. Both carriers provide jet service to Cairns, Townsville, Proserpine, Mackay and Rockhampton. (Service to Gladstone for Heron Island or Bundaberg for Lady Elliot requires transfer to a regional or local carrier and is not by jet.) The disadvantage of this service agreement to the traveller frequently is a lack of competitive choices for times of departure. The advantage is that, should one carrier be fully booked, the other may have seats available. While both companies provide friendly, safe and reasonably on-time service, there are some minor differences between Australian Airlines and Ansett. For shorter runs, Ansett operates principally with Boeing 737s while Australian Airlines uses chiefly DC9s with a few 727s. The 737 seating is six across (three and three), while the DC9 is five across (three and two). For longer hauls, Australian Airlines uses Airbus A300s while Ansett has Boeing 767s.

Occasionally the carriers will use different routes to the same destination. For example, on the day Australian Airlines — then called TAA — flew from Sydney to Cairns (1228 miles direct) with a stop in Brisbane, Ansett offered service to Cairns with the stop in Townsville. The result was that the Ansett flight saved about a hundred miles and arrived almost two hours before the TAA service. It is worth checking (and re-checking after you arrive in Australia) to see exactly what service is available for the day you want to travel.

Australians will tell you continually how expensive their domestic travel is — in fact a subject of debate in national election campaigns — and they are right. We know of people who found it less expensive to travel transcontinentally to Perth from Brisbane via Singapore rather than fly directly! Many Sydneyites select Fiji over the barrier reef for holidays because of low-cost packages. (Both Australians and Americans find an extra inducement from the fact that Air Pacific, Qantas' international Fiji subsidiary, also periodically offers a "Pacific Air Pass" allowing trips from Fiji to Vanuatu, Tonga and Samoa for about a third of the usual airfare.)

Americans, however, are not without remedy. Both Ansett and Australian Airlines discount their fairs thirty percent for Americans. You must either purchase these tickets in the United States in conjunction with your travel arrangements to Australia or, if buying the tickets in Australia, must present inbound air tickets showing that you arrived on an excursion or incentive fare basis (and you may be asked to show your passport). Currently the only other condition is that you must travel on the domestic airline at least 1000 kilometers — 600 miles — to qualify for the discount.

If you wish to change domestic air carriers after your tickets have been issued, Australian airlines don't automatically accept each other's tickets as most do in the U.S. You must first go to the airline desk for the company on which you are ticketed and get an endorsement — which they will issue right there without any fuss — and then go to the counter of the company you want to fly with. While it takes only an extra minute to get the endorsement, at larger airports the Australian Airlines and Ansett desks are some distance apart — in fact in separate buildings at Kingsford Smith airport in Sydney, and it may take you fifteen or twenty minutes to get the tickets validated. It is wise, therefore, to allow extra time at the airport if you have switched airlines.

The principal air terminals with jet service in North Queensland from north to south are Cairns and Townsville (which have international air service as well), Proserpine, Mackay and Rockhampton.

Air Distances between Major Cities (miles)

Cooktown - Cairns   107
Cairns - Townsville 177
Cairns - Brisbane   865
Cairns - Sydney   1228
Townsville - Proserpine 145
Townsville - Brisbane   692
Townsville - Sydney 1051
Proserpine - Mackay 63
Mackay-Rockhampton 174
Rockhampton - Gladstone   59
Gladston-Brisbane 271
Brisbane - Sydney   450
Brisbane-Melbourne 857

Within Queensland, the principal air carrier is Air Queensland (the newish name for BPA or Bush Pilots Airline, a colorful and accurately descriptive name which in our estimation should not have been changed because they continue to be charmingly bush-league in several respects). Recently this carrier was acquired by Australian Airlines, although present plans are to continue separate operation. By a strange accident of fate, the line had contracted with Australian Airlines' competitor, Ansett, to use the Ansett computer system for its reservations operations, so for the next year a Australian Airlines company will be booking through Ansett's computers.

Omitting only a Cairns-Townsville route, and operating several familiar species of prop aircraft, Air Queensland connects all of the major cities and towns of Queensland, including service to Gladstone and Cooktown. Expansion plans call for purchase of a   new generation of French jet-prop aircraft in the near future.

In addition, this carrier operates direct air service to several of the resorts: Brampton Island (daily from Mackay), Dunk Island (daily except Monday and Thursday from Cairns, and daily from Townsville), Hamilton Island (occasional service from Cairns, Mackay and Townsville), and Lizard Island (daily except Thursday from Cairns). Currently Air Queensland flights from Cairns may   operate through TAA, or through Ansett, or through their own terminal at the general aviation airport which is over a mile to the north. Be sure to call and find out which terminal they're using for your flight, or you could end up carrying your luggage quite a way.

Reef World Airline — formerly known as Air Whitsunday —offers scheduled air service linking its home base, midway between Airlie Beach and Shute Harbor (just a few miles from Proserpine), with Mackay and Townsville. It also has scheduled seaplane service to Orpheus and Hinchinbrook Islands. In fact, because this plane stops at both islands, it is the only scheduled air link available between two Great Barrier Reef resorts without having to go back to the coast. Air Queensland has service from Lizard Island to Cairns, continuing on to Dunk Island; while a convenient connection, this does involve returning to a gateway city. Similarly, from Whitsunday Field, Reef World also offers seaplane service to the resorts of the Whitsunday Group on a charter basis, and occasional scheduled flights as well, using 3-passenger Lake Buccaneers or 13-passenger Grumman Mallards, so there are through connections possible from Hinchinbrook and Orpheus to the Whitsunday Group.

Many small air services operate from the coast serving various island resorts. For example, Lindeman Aerial Service from Mackay serves its namesake resort, and Hamilton Air Services operates helicopters for reef excursions and small planes for   charter and regular service to Mackay and other gateways.   Sunstate connects Rockhampton and Great Keppel Island with 15-minute flights, and Helitrans operates helicopter service to Heron Island out of Gladstone airport.

We concluded that there currently are insufficient practical boat connections from gateway cities to the Barrier Reef resorts. From Cairns there is scheduled service to Green Island several times a day and excursion service to Fitzroy Island along with Green, but these are mainly day trips.   Dunk Island is served by water taxi from Mission Beach, and Hinchinbrook from Cardwell. From Townsville, there are regular ferries to Magnetic Island. Heron Island has launch service from Gladstone.   In the Whitsunday Group, there are ferries from Shute Harbor to many of the area resorts (although getting to Shute Harbor will require bus or taxi service from Proserpine or Whitsunday Field).   Otherwise boat connections are intermittent and poor, schedules change, and prices are so high that notwithstanding the cost the time savings of flying almost always are most persuasive.

This is not to say that you will not find many references to launch and ferry connections in Australian Tourist Commission publications. What we mean is that you should keep a map handy when referring to travel promotion literature about Queensland. You may read, for example, that there is launch service to Dunk Island from Clump Point. The problem is that Clump Point is not   really a place; it is a jetty several miles from Mission Beach and reachable by once or twice a day bus service along the coast or by taxi from the town — which itself is not regularly served by any scheduled air service and is about midway between Cairns and Townsville. Similarly there is regular ferry service between Great Keppel Island and Rosslyn Bay, which is many miles and a difficult journey from the nearest scheduled air service at   Rockhampton — fine for locals, but difficult for visiting Americans.

Within single groups of nearby islands it is sometimes possible to arrange boat connections. Since fuel costs for ocean boating are not inconsequential, however, charter fees may prove high. Moreover such connections are sometimes very weather sensitive, for you are now leaving the sheltered bays of island resorts and crossing open waters where tides and winds may influence whether a particular type of boat can make the journey comfortably.

It takes just under an hour for a launch to travel between Dunk Island and Hinchinbrook Island. (It took the staff at the reception desk longer than that to think of a way of getting between the two resorts without going back to the coast and renting a car.) There is no organized service connecting these resorts, so you must hire a water taxi for the trip if you wish to go directly. One water taxi company out of Mission Beach serving Dunk Island didn't want to make this trip. The other two taxis gave us quotes, and the low tariff for our trip was a rather stiff $A160. The advantage was that the connection cut out an extra day of travel and incidentally offered a beautiful sea trip past several islands along the way. With this in mind, the price for two was not that unreasonable, considering that there would also have been water taxi and ground transportation costs to make the same connection by returning to the coast.

While many resorts commonly offer day charters which visit other islands, the boat transportation services connecting resort islands are quite rare and require special arrangements. The particular significance for visitors from a great distance is the fact that direct inter-island transit is still very undeveloped, and stringing together a series of resort visits is rather complicated.

There is regular bus service along the Queensland coast. This is generally more advisable for coastal sightseeing, rather than island hopping. Locals scoffed at the idea of relying upon rail connections, although they ostensibly do exist. There are car rental agencies (multi-nationals such as Hertz, Avis and Budget, as well as local companies) in all of the major cities and towns of Queensland, but be sure to book ahead during the busy holiday seasons. Your U.S. or Canadian driver's license is accepted for holiday driving in Australia. Drop-off charges are not as bad as in the United States. (Expect to pay about $A50 per day for a small car, including mandatory insurance charges.) The Bruce Highway along the Queensland coast is well paved and graded two-lane road. Don't expect U.S.-style freeways, however. It is by no means straight and curves about as much as the coastline. You should also anticipate considerable slow agricultural traffic. Driving time is accordingly somewhat longer than you might expect for comparable U.S. trips.

In planning your journey to and between islands, keep the distances in mind. Although not unreasonable by American standards, they are longer than you might expect since Australia is a very large country. For most Americans wishing to plan an easy vacation, it will probably prove simplest to select a resort or combination of resorts with reasonable air access. If you enjoy the adventure and some awfully scenic launch or light plane trips, however, arranging your own way as you go (since advance bookings will be virtually impossible) is fairly easy — if a tad pricey, and you will find the Queenslanders anxious to facilitate your journey as best they can.

Attire

Life at all Great Barrier Reef resorts is very informal. This means different things at different islands, however. At Orpheus Island, for example they do ask that bathing suits be the minimum attire unless you seek out one of their more secluded beaches. On the other hand, at this elegant resort many people choose to dress rather nicely for dinner.

Expect to wear shorts or a bathing suit all day and light tropical clothes in the evening. Tee shirts or beach covers are vital in the daytime for sun protection and the occasional rain shower. Buy a souvenir hat or sun visor there. Bring a pair of comfortable sandals or thongs. Sand and paved walk ways get very hot in the direct tropical sun and, especially if your feet are sensitive, it can be miserable walking from room to beach or boat across the desert sand.

Some resorts have dress-up nights. A few others are unconcerned if you wear your bathing suit to the dinner table. Guests at most seem to have set a relaxed standard of unpretentious informal dress for dinner. Although we have tried to give you a feel for each of the resorts, if you plan to visit more than one you should plan to bring suitable light casual evening wear. The temperature is most commonly such (except very occasionally during the winter — June and July — when there may be tropical breezes or very occasional stormy winds) that you rarely will want to wear long sleeves even in the evening unless you are at one of the few air conditioned resort dining rooms or want to dress up a bit.

For men, any shirt with collar (and we definitely recommend short sleeves for most evenings because of the temperature and humidity) will generally do. Short sleeve dress shirts and pull-over golf-type shirts are equally acceptable, worn with cotton or linen slacks or walking shorts (but in the case of shorts, all resorts requested that gentlemen wear long socks.) We saw some blue jeans, but lighter weights and lighter colors were worn by the overwhelming majority. Jackets are not required and were only rarely seen.

For women, light blouses or tops with a wrap around or similar casual skirt or slacks and open shoes are just fine. Cottons and synthetics greatly outnumbered silks, presumably because of the presence of laundries and the absence of dry cleaning facilities on virtually all of the islands. Stockings were a matter of personal preference and by no means universal.

Don't overpack. Perhaps because tipping is rare in Australia (airport porters are paid a flat rate per piece carried), there aren't a lot of porters around. You may find you have to hustle your own bags between airlines and perhaps a bit more than when travelling in the U.S. or Europe. We have now taken to carrying a heavy duty collapsible suitcase trolley with us wherever we travel, and we were particularly happy we had it in Australia. The less you pack, the less you carry — and the more room you have in your suitcase for souvenirs.

Every resort sells tee shirts for anywhere from $A8 to $A16, depending on quality and fabric, and they make fine souvenirs. There are some very nice and quite unusual pure cotton shirts made in China and others from Singapore in styles we had not seen anywhere else. There are also tee shirt "dresses", over-long pullovers, which women can wear either belted or unbelted as poolside coverups or for informal evening wear, ranging in price from $A10 to $A30, again depending on style and fabric. If you wish, you can acquire much of what you might need for daytime wear as you go along.

Since you live in bathing suits and sandals at most resorts, neither men nor women need as much in the way of underwear and socks or stockings as for other vacations. Australians commonly wear shorts with long socks and shoes as town business attire during the day; such dress is perfectly appropriate (and far more comfortable than long trousers in the heat) for travel throughout Queensland — on airplanes, boats, in cities and towns, and certainly at any resort (where you will delete the socks and shoes during the day). The availability of free or coin laundries at most of the resorts means you don't even have to rely on hand washing if you plan to be away for any length of time. Most resorts provide irons either in the room or with the laundry facilities, so you can even look well pressed if you wish.

In winter (June-August) one sweater or lightweight jacket may be comfortable and useful in the event of occasional cooler balmy evening breezes. You will never have occasion to need fancy dress shoes. Men should have a comfortable and versatile pair of shoes for walking and evening wear — perhaps topsiders or some other similar boating or sport shoes — and a pair of tennis or jogging shoes which doubles for walking, reef exploring and casual wear. Inexpensive resort shoes in whites or beige are more than adequate for evenings at the nicest resorts, and they have the added virtue of being lighter and easier to pack. Women may want another pair of sandals to be worn in the evening, tennis or jogging shoes, and a good walking shoe, but dressy high heels are rarely seen.

Resort stores generally all had at least a basic selection of toiletries, and all offered at least a limited selection of vacation wear suitable for the particular resort for those who arrived without suitable clothing. Sun lotions are abundantly available, albeit slightly expensive, and insect repellant is plentiful. On the other hand, such items as contact lens solutions, varied brands of cosmetics, or even antihistamines (for the cold we brought with us on the airplane) and other over-the-counter remedies were scarce, although they were much more readily available at chemist shops in coastal towns such as Cairns and Townsville. Unless you are planning to travel extensively along the coast, however, you had better plan to bring important personal items along with you.

Photography

Photographic opportunities abound, so bring your favorite camera. Remember that tropical daylight is intensely bright, so beware of "backlighting" — that's when the scene you're shooting has a lot of light behind it, when your foreground is dark and the background is light. These situations invariably trick your automatic light meter and give you pictures with murky dark subject matter and a bright burst of background light. Remember to set the light meter on the main subject of your picture and not on the sun reflecting off water or the intensely bright sky.

As with any vacation resort, familiar brands of film are readily available and expensive. There are even one-day processing stores in most coastal towns and all major cities. If you bring film, most professionals recommend that you carry it in readily available lead lined film bags to protect it against airport x-ray examination (which is used sporadically in Australia for passengers boarding jet flights).

If you intend to dive or snorkel, you won't ever forgive yourself if you don't bring some sort of underwater camera. Your choices begin with a relatively inexpensive camera — either an instamatic model (Minolta or Hanimex instamatic type in the under $125 range), or the Hanimex or Canon underwater 35 mm. (around $250). As an alternative you may elect a simple underwater housing (Ewa, price around $50, to more sophisticated equipment in the $200 range) for an instamatic or other camera which allows you to take your regular camera to sea. For the serious photographer there is the Nikonos V (camera and lens around $500), which will cost closer to $1000 when the ensemble is completed with proper flash equipment. The most exciting advance is the development of (currently very expensive) underwater video cameras!

Remember that virtually all underwater photography is either fast film (ASA 400 or faster) or flash photography because water of any depth quickly begins to filter color and intensity out of sunlight. For battery operated flash units, you may be using quite a bit of electricity so may want to bring one or more spare sets of batteries along depending on how fast you go through film. Also bear in mind that underwater shots capture color only if within five feet or so of the subject. You may want to buy a pamphlet on this type of photography if you aren't familiar with its peculiarities.

Getting ready

What do you need to do to get ready, aside from packing your clothes, to have a perfect trip? Don't forget your passport. Americans also must obtain an Australian visa from their embassy in Washington or one of their consular offices. (A list of consular offices is included at the end of Chapter 8.) If you appear in person with a photograph, the process generally takes one day. If you have them send you an application and mail it to them with a return envelope, expect it to take two weeks or longer. The visas are good for trips up to six months in length and are valid for two years.

If you haven't prepared for the sun adequately, or if you otherwise require medical assistance, you will have to pay for your health care since (as you would probably assume) Australian national health insurance does not cover foreign visitors. Currently, of all the Great Barrier Reef resorts, only Outrigger Resort on Hamilton Island has a resident physician. The others have dispensaries or nursing care available and arrange for health care with mainland physicians. As far as prescription medication, you can legally   bring up to four week's supply of prescription medicine into Australia without a doctor's certificate authorizing a larger amount.   An endorsement by an Australian doctor for a prescription issued in North America will enable an Australian pharmacist to fill a prescription in Australia.

That's it!   You are travelling to a place much like home, and there's virtually nothing you might be planning to carry along that you can't lay your hands on somehow in Cairns, Townsville, and especially Sydney or Melbourne.

Strangler Fig on Hinchinbrook Island

Hamilton Island

Things to Know
•weather
•measurements
•telling time
•calling Australia

Weather & Seasons

When you cross the equator, the seasons are reversed. Therefore while we shiver in December, Australians enjoy their summer, and it's a peculiar experience to see Santa Claus in short sleeves and lightweight clothes. On the other hand, Australia's modest ski season is at its peak in July or August. The Great Barrier Reef region is firmly in tropical climes, however. Because the winds in tropical latitudes tend to travel to where the sun is directly overhead, and during the Barrier Reef's winter the sun is far to the north over the Tropic of Cancer, this is when the Reef's climate is in its most benign mood, from late April through to September or October, and this is when many southern Australians escape their own winter and migrate to the North Queensland coast. June and July are also when Australian schools — including those in Queensland — take mid-year holidays of a week or two resulting in greater crowding on some islands, more demand for rental cars, and some fully booked resorts. (If your travel agent doesn't have this year's dates for *school holidays,* do check with the Queensland National Tourist Bureau in New York or Los Angeles if you are planning any part of your Barrier Reef trip without reservations.)

In summer (January to March) the sun is over the Tropic of Capricorn, actually south of much of the Barrier Reef area, creating distinctly tropical weather patterns for the islands. Sudden heavy rain storms are possible, and thunderstorms can stir up brief, wild winds. Nonetheless the weather is generally hot and pleasant, and many Queenslanders (in addition to a substantial population of southerners) plan their Christmas and New Years holidays at the Reef's resorts.

Apart from the statistically remote possibility of a hurricane (every few years, usually with several days' warning) and the few humid summer months, the Reef weather is usually beautiful. Periods of high humidity are common in the summer wet season (again, remember this means

February), but rain is by no means a constant phenomenon during this period. Often it may rain for a part of a day and then clear. Occasionally in February or March it storms for as long as a few days and then clears. In any event it tends to remain quite warm, and the rain is frequently a welcome respite from the temperatures of the tropical summer. As with most resorts in the tropics, the optimum time to travel for best weather conditions in the minds of many experienced travellers is usually spring or fall — which in Australia would be around October-November and April-May, when weather conditions in the islands are generally sunny and brushed by languid light winds.

Resort Weather on the Great Barrier Reef
(monthly highs, lows, average rainfall)

	Jan	Feb	Mar	Apr	May	Jun	July	Aug	Sep	Oct	Nov	Dec
highs	89	88	87	84	81	78	77	80	82	85	87	88
lows	74	75	72	71	68	65	62	64	66	69	72	74
rainfall (inches)	15.7	17.4	18.3	7.0	3.6	2.0	1.2	1.0	1.4	1.4	3.3	6.7

Average total sunshine hours per month
July-January 220;
February-June 190

Average daily mean humidity: 75-80%

Measurements

Australia uses the metric system for weights, measures and temperature. They used to use feet and inches, so Australians often express distances in miles as well as kilometers, yards as well as meters, and will understand you when you do too. So you will know, however, you can quickly approximate American measurements if you multiply kilometers by .6 to calculate miles, centimeters by 2.5 to get inches, and meters by .9 to get yards. Kilograms are 2.2 pounds, so you can jump on the airline baggage scale and convince yourself you haven't gained an ounce. You very occasionally may see a few weights expressed in the English measurement of *stone;* these are 14 pounds, and we don't know any easy way to multiply by 14.

Australians refer to liters, rather than quarts and gallons, but so long as you remember that a liter is roughly a quart — 1.057 quarts to be more precise, but close enough for buying wine — you can get by just fine. Gasoline is generally sold by the liter, so don't applaud the amazingly low prices until you multiply them by 3.8 to convert to our familiar gallon prices.

Of all measurements familiar to us, Australians are least familiar with the fahrenheit temperature scale, so you should be prepared to speak Centigrade with them. When you hear the high temperature forecast for the day is 30, instead of reaching for a sweater you should be shedding most of your clothes — it's going to hit 86 fahrenheit.

    Centigrade 20 25 30 35   40
    Fahrenheit 68 77 86 95 104

To calculate fahrenheit from centigrade, divide the centigrade reading by 5, multiply by 9, and add 32 to the total. Every 10ª centigrade is 18ª fahrenheit.

Incidentally, don't expect long range weather forecasts for northern Queensland. Australia depends heavily on U.S. satellite data for weather information, and by the time it reaches Australia and gets interpreted for the southern hemisphere, it isn't sufficiently long-range any more. Particularly for limited population areas like the Barrier Reef region, there isn't the type of several days' advance prediction we have get in the United States. This inability to predict tomorrow's high temperatures obviously won't affect your vacation particularly, but it does create a more uncertain situation for yachters who want to plan ahead but can't always tell from whence the next day's winds will blow.

Telling Time

From the Pacific Coast between November and April, Queensland is +18 hours relative to Pacific standard time. The easiest way to convert is to subtract 6 hours from West Coast time and add a full day. When the United States is on daylight savings time from May through October the Great Barrier Reef is +17 hours, or convert by subtracting 7 and adding a full day. The reason for this seeming anomaly — that when we set our clocks ahead for daylight time we actually reduce the time difference between ourselves and Queensland is that time is determined relative to Universal Mean Time in Greenwich, England; we are behind UMT and come an hour closer when we go on daylight savings, while Australia is ahead of UMT, so our daylight time catches us up an hour on the Australians.

To confuse matters further, much of Australia — including Sydney, Melbourne, and most major cities outside Queensland — observes daylight saving time during their summer months. Sydney is then +19 — subtract 5 and add a day — when they are on daylight savings time and we are off (November to March), +18 — subtract 6 and add a day — when both Australia and the U.S. are on daylight savings time, and +17 — subtract 7 and add a day — when we are on daylight savings time and they are off (May through October).

These calculations are all given from the West Coast. For other time zones in the United States, diminish the hourly difference accordingly (remember, you are closer to Greenwich, England, as you move eastward across the U.S.); when the Barrier Reef is +18 hours ahead of San Francisco, it is +17 to Denver, +16 to Chicago and +15 to New York. If this is all too much bother, consult the chart, lie on the beach, and leave your watch at home.

U.S. and Barrier Reef Time Difference
(U.S. not on daylight time)

San Francisco	Denver	Chicago	New York	Barrier Reef
[Monday]	[Monday]	[Monday]	[Monday]	[Tuesday]
6:00 am	7:00 am	8:00 am	9:00 am	midnight
8:00 am	9:00 am	10:00 am	11:00 am	2:00 am
10:00 am	11:00 am	noon	1:00 pm	4:00 am
noon	1:00 pm	2:00 pm	3:00 pm	6:00 am
2:00 pm	3:00 pm	4:00 pm	5:00 pm	8:00 am
4:00 pm	5:00 pm	6:00 pm	7:00 pm	10:00 am
6:00 pm	7:00 pm	8:00 pm	9:00 pm	noon
8:00 pm	9:00 pm	10:00 pm	11:00 pm	2:00 pm
10:00 pm	11:00 pm	*midnight	*1:00 am	4:00 am
*midnight	*1:00 am	*2:00 am	*3:00 am	6:00 pm

(U.S. on daylight time)

San Francisco	Denver	Chicago	New York	Barrier Reef
[Monday]	[Monday]	[Monday]	[Monday]	[Tuesday]
6:00 am	7:00 am	8:00 am	9:00 am	*11:00 pm
8:00 am	9:00 am	10:00 am	11:00 am	1:00 am
10:00 am	11:00 am	noon	1:00 pm	3:00 am
noon	1:00 pm	2:00 pm	3:00 pm	5:00 am
2:00 pm	3:00 pm	4:00 pm	5:00 pm	7:00 am
4:00 pm	5:00 pm	6:00 pm	7:00 pm	9:00 am
6:00 pm	7:00 pm	8:00 pm	9:00 pm	11:00 am
8:00 pm	9:00 pm	10:00 pm	11:00 pm	1:00 pm
10:00 pm	11:00 pm	*midnight	*1:00 am	3:00 pm
*midnight	*1:00 am	*2:00 am	*3:00 am	5:00 pm

* indicates same day in U.S. and Barrier Reef

Calling Australia

Telephone connections between the United States and Australia are excellent. Considering how long it often takes mail to reach the far north coast of Australia, investing $10 or so in phone calls can be well worth it, especially considering the almost invariably very friendly reception Americans get when calling the Great Barrier Reef area.

For U.S. cities having international direct dialing service (IDDS), Australia is easily and quickly reached by dialing 011 61. The *international access code* is 011, and Australia's *country code* is 61. Then dial the Australian area code — numbers in North Queensland are generally area code 70 to 79. (Note that in Australia you may see the area code written as *070* because in other parts of the country they have one-, two- and three-number area codes, but in dialing from the US, that initial *0* in their area code is omitted.) Lastly, dial the five to seven digit (in northern Queensland, usually six digit) local number. For example, to call the Queensland Government Tourist Bureau in Cairns (assuming the one in Los Angeles can't help you), simply dial 011 61 70 51 3588#. The U.S. telephone company recommends that # at the end of the number on touch-tone phones to speed the call through.

It is generally quite easy to call from Australia to the United States. From the larger cities, most hotel rooms have telephones permitting direct dialing with charges added to your hotel bill. Calls are billed at what are called *standard hotel* and not telephone company rates, so anticipate rather heavy surcharges; the usual $A2 per minute becomes approximately $A4 per minute, but calls generally go though with no delay and connections are reasonably clear. We did encounter substantial difficulties, however, having calls billed to our United States telephone credit cards, although we were continually assured that it could be done if we would just wait until arrangements were made. It was much faster and easier just to make the calls and pay for them there.

Australian pay phones, incidentally, are somewhat different than ours, but are pretty clearly explained on the instructions at each station, so no need to feel intimidated. Just make sure you have a handful of 20 cent coins and you will have little difficulty. International pay phones, labeled ISD, also take the hexagonal 50 cent coins and permit you to make your call to the U.S. at telcom rates. You will have to get used to a different set of dial and busy signals, but that's easy enough. One nice thing on the newer phones: you deposit your coins and, after your party answers, meters on the phone calculate the charges during your call and display how much money you have left on your toll call.

Hayman Island—west wing reception patio

Dunk Island

Lifestyle
•*food & drink*
•*tipping*
•*amenities*
•*money & credit*
•*prices & packages*

Food and Drink

The Great Barrier Reef area offers some excellent culinary and gustatory opportunities. All food is very edible. Health standards are enforced at a very high level. Quality beef, lamb, shellfish and seafood are available, and most (although regrettably not all) resorts and local restaurants serve the finest ingredients.

Resort breakfast generally is English style with selections of meats, toasts, pancakes, fish, bacon, sausages and the like in addition to fruits, juices and cereals. Lunches are served at the table at a few of the smaller resorts but more generally are buffet style. Dinners are generally four course (or larger) affairs: soup, entree (which in Australia is an introductory course), main course and dessert.

You will find a fine selection of fresh tropical fruits to begin the day and with most meals. North Queensland is rich in mango particularly. There is also abundant banana, pineapple, paw paw (papaya), kiwi and passion fruit. While coconut appears to grow abundantly, it is not commonly served or used in Australian cuisine.

There are several things, in particular different types of seafood, which are somewhat new to most Americans but which are close relatives to familiar U.S. dishes and are an absolute must on a Barrier Reef trip. *Bugs* (also called Bay Lobster) from Moreton Bay near Brisbane in South Queensland are an odd-shaped but exquisite scampi-sized lobster (rarely over 6" in total length including their strange flat head) prepared just like their larger cousins and eaten by removing the shell and feasting on the tail. This delicacy was discovered in the 1950s when new methods of trawling for prawns were devised. Only later was it recognized that these were not the unpleasant tasting Balmain bugs but were a delicious new find. Up until then these small creatures were in such abundance they were considered a nuisance and were often thrown away rather than consumed. The Moreton Bay bugs are particularly memorable when grilled simply and served with a garlic butter sauce.

If you've ever enjoyed the hard shell Dungeness crab of which San Franciscans are so proud, you'll love the   Queensland mud crabs, one of Australia's biggest crustaceans, occasionally growing to four pounds. Don't be put off by the "mud" in their name; they're generally found in the   mangrove tree swamps and are also called mangrove crab. These delicious creatures are about the same size as the Pacific Coast variety, have large bodies and major claws but lack the smaller meaty legs of the American variety. Although Australians serve these crabs either hot or cold, they are particularly superb cold with either mayonnaise or melted butter accompanied by a new Australian chablis or chardonnay or, if you prefer beer, one of the light Queensland lagers.

Queensland is fresh prawn country. Prawn trawlers can be seen working the channels and bays up and down the coast, and many of them sell part of their catch to nearby resort kitchens before snap-freezing the rest right aboard the fishing boat, The frozen catch is processed and then shipped all over the world. Australians most often serve   their fresh prawns whole — whether hot or cold, so don't be surprised to see head and tails, and expect to do a bit of peeling work in the eating process. The trawlers also often bring in abundant catches of small squid, so the restaurants frequently offer fried or sauteed calamari.

The Australian rock lobster tail which has become almost a cliché item on American restaurant menus comes from the south, quite a distance from the Barrier Reef, and may not be available fresh in the north. (Some friends of ours even had trouble finding it fresh in Sydney and were told it was virtually all being exported to the U.S.) From closer to the north coast, however, there are very similar crayfish which are almost indistinguishable from the southern variety. Either makes a superb lobster dinner.

The barramundi is probably one of the best cooking fish in the world, a moderately large fish caught in northern Australian rivers, with thick succulent fillets. A close runner-up is the coral trout which you may catch in the waters off many Barrier Reef islands. There are also   excellent coral salmon and bass. Slightly more abundant is the sweetlip which in some areas are so common they will almost take a hook without bait.

Large mackerel are also common, especially in the Whitsunday Passage. Even the dishes served as "fresh reef fish", translated as whatever the fishing crew caught this morning, are a complete pleasure.

Beef is a major product of Queensland which boasts some of the largest cattle "stations" in the world. Interestingly we found less chicken or other poultry then one would expect, and the lamb — although locally produced — is more commonly served on the breakfast hot table, and we felt it was almost invariably poorly prepared. We were impressed by the quality of the locally grown vegetables from the tablelands west and south of Cairns. Desserts are of the familiar variety and generally quite enjoyable, although we didn't particularly cotton to the Pavlova, which we were told is the "national dessert". It's a mixture of meringue and whipped cream, very rich but equally monotonous.

Australian beers are known world-wide. The local brew in the far north is Cairns' NQ (North Queensland) Lager, although as you proceed south among the islands more people seem to prefer the 4-X from Brisbane, Carlton or Victoria Bitter, or two beers which are most familiar to Americans, Fosters and Swans. With recently enacted very strict "drink-driving" laws, Australians who have to drive after a meal are turning to a new generation of specially brewed very low alcohol beers.

Many Americans are unaware that Australia is a major wine producing nation with an abundance of quality products well worth becoming acquainted with. Australians do tend to drink their wines quite young, so don't be surprised if you're offered a wine bearing a label with the same vintage as the date on your plane ticket. Their principle wine growing regions are to the south: Hunter Valley (around 130 miles north of Sydney), Griffith area (400 miles from Sydney), Barossa Valley (starting 30 miles northeast of Adlelaide) and Swan Valley (north-east of Perth). Less well known are Rutherglen and the Goulburn Valley (near Melbourne) and the Clare and Watervale districts (20 miles north of Adelaide).

Australian varietals include some familiar and some less well known in the United States. Among whites, their chablis is much closer to the French product, with less body but possessing a hearty chardonnay character, and fortunately bearing no relationship to the often dismal California wine using the same title. Australian chardonnays, on the other hand, have much of the bold fruitiness associated with California chardonnays generally without the earthy character of the traditional French white burgundies.

The most common Australian "house white" is called a riesling, although in fact it is commonly produced chiefly from semillon grapes. (Australia is starting to produce a   true riesling, but these are not yet widely offered.) Some bars also offer a domestic mosel by the glass or carafe, but this is generally far too sweet for most people's taste. The bulk riesling, though, is generally very acceptable — indeed much more so than many wines served routinely in bars and restaurants in the U.S. — and is quite modest in price.

As for reds, Australian wines need a bit more development in our opinion. A good Aussie shiraz (also   sometimes labeled Hermitage) can be a pleasant find, and we enjoyed a couple of their young light pinot noirs. The cabernet sauvignon in our estimation, however, needs more development before they will share the limelight with their California or Bordeaux cousins.

In addition to the general selection of drinks in your room refrigerator, the dining rooms and bars will be pleased to sell you drink supplies to take to your room. At many resorts you can if you wish buy a box of riesling to put in the refrigerator. Yes, we said "box", for it is Australia which has appears to have dominated the industry which markets bulk wine in cardboard boxes with reinforced foil liners. At $A10 for four liters — remember, that's about a gallon — the wine is really quite inexpensive yet surprisingly drinkable.

All of the resorts are "fully licensed" (unlike some restaurants in towns and even large cities, where you must bring your own drinks) and generally have full bar and wine and beer selections. Drinks are very fairly priced by U.S. standards ($A0.80 - $A1.25 for a glass of wine at the bar), and the bartenders will keep a running tab for guests during their stay.

Tipping

Almost all Australians — perhaps excepting people in service industries — like the fact that theirs is not a tipping society. They hope visiting Americans won't ruin it for them. No service charges are added to restaurant or hotel bills.

The typical Australian does not tip for normal meal service. If he or she wants to recognize special service, it is generally accepted that 10% of the bill is very sufficient. Australians hardly ever tip a taxi driver unless special help is rendered with luggage or some other difficulty. Hotel bellmen are salaried and will deliver bags to your room without sticking their hands out for a gratuity; say "thank you" and they will depart. Airport porters charge per piece carried and do not expect a tip from Australians. (Most airports have ample free baggage wagons, so porters are becoming quite scarce.)

Everyone, however, has learned that Americans do tip, so a fraction of your drivers, porters and waiters may linger to give you the chance to follow your custom rather than theirs. Don't be intimidated; tip if you wish, but don't feel it is required to conform to local custom.

Amenities

About a third of the Great Barrier Reef resorts have television sets or radios in the rooms. Few have an alarm clock. Then again, who needs alarm clocks when one of nature's best alarms, an incredible array of tropical birds, announces the dawn for all who want to be up and about during the coolest part of the day. If you are interested in having a radio — and listening both to Queensland's AM radio stations out of Cairns, Townsville, Mackay or Brisbane is both fun and informative — consider bringing a small shirt-pocket size AM battery operated radio.

If you want to be more tuned in to the world and listen to Radio Australia and other national shortwave broadcasts to and from the southeastern part of the world, consider buying one of the newer battery operated radios which effectively pick up AM, FM and short wave yet weigh only a matter of ounces. Prices for these technological wonders in the U.S. range from about $75 to $250 depending on refinements, including such things as automatic shut-off and digital clocks which make the small wonder into a fine clock radio which you may be able to make good use of at home.

A few resorts have telephones in the rooms. Daydream Island does but goes through a central switchboard. Hayman, South Molle and Hamilton Islands have dial telephones in the rooms. (All four of these resorts are in the Whitsunday Group.) Dunk and South Molle have two pay phones at each resort; at both the reception offices close at 5:00, so incoming phone calls must be arranged during business hours. Deluxe Orpheus Island has but one phone on the entire island; located in the office it is shared by reception, management and guests. Lizard Island goes one better; it has only a single radio telephone at the desk.

At the island resorts without room phones, if you are expecting incoming calls, advise the staff; in most   instances they will be very cooperative in allowing you to receive brief calls in the office. For the most part, however, these are distinctly not resorts where you can keep in close touch with the office and are for those who want to leave such things behind — but then that's why you're travelling 7500 miles or more, isn't it?

Hamilton Island

At some resorts, you are given a room key at check in time (a few resorts don't even bother), but you will   never use it at most, so you might as well leave it in the   room at all but the very largest hotels. Only in one particularly large resort did we even hear of even a hint of a problem, and that involved staff and resort property rather than any guest possessions. Australians do not appear particularly security conscious, and we saw no reason for them to be so in most vacation areas.

Electricity throughout Australia is 240/250 volts. Australia uses a unique three-pronged plug for its appliances;   the bottom vertical prong is the ground and the top two are the "hot" plugs. If your appliances are grounded and do not pose a shock risk, you can get by using just the top two prongs.   These top two are what make Australia so different; they look like they started with an American plug then twisted the bottom of each prong to the outside about 30 degrees. Best not to try twisting your appliance   plugs to fit their sockets, particularly since most American appliances now have one prong larger than the other because we build in our grounds differently. Your appliance plug may not fit their socket, and you could have a messed up situation when you return home.

Electronic supply stores and appliance stores catering to international clientele carry adapters which will let you plug in your hair dryer, radio or whatever in Australia. If you have bought an international converter set, it probably came with one of these widgets. Call your nearest Australian consulate or national tourist office if you can't track one down in your home town. Do, however, try to bring at least one with you, since hotels and resorts never seem to have any available.

Otherwise, Australian and particularly Barrier Reef amenities are much like home. Everything is very clean by our standards. Bathrooms ranging in degrees of luxury from plain to outstanding are as you would expect them in   comparable northern hemisphere facilities from national parks to exotic resorts. (Outrigger Resort at Hamilton Island, Lizard Island and Hayman Resort, for example, provide wall-mounted electric hair dryers in every bathroom — something we had not previously seen in the U.S. or Europe.) Most resorts provide electric irons, either in the room or in conjunction with laundry facilities, so you do not need that travel iron. One thing virtually every Australian resort offers — it must be a law — is an electric pot for heating water for instant coffee or tea in your room and an ample supply of both.

Money and Credit

The Australian dollar ($A), like the U.S. counterpart,   is 100 cents. There are coins worth 1, 2, 5, 10, 20 and 50 cents (the last a fascinating 12-sided coin identical in size and shape to the Fijiian 50 cent), as well as a gold-colored $1 coin. Australian currency comes in 2, 5, 10, 20, 50 and 100 dollar bills of differing colors. You can, if you wish, acquire Australian currency and Australian dollar travellers' checks in the United States from Thomas Cook offices or most any urban currency exchange. Sydney's Kingsford-Smith airport has a large banking facility just as you exit customs. Cairns' airport, however, has much more limited facilities, and the bank could be closed when you arrive.

Every resort accepted more than one of the familiar major credit cards. Lizard Island wants American Express or Diners, but Visa and Mastercard were accepted everywhere else as well. As a practical matter, there is little need to carry   cash or credit cards with you while on the resort premises. Everything in the way of food, drink, supplies, souvenirs and excursions can be charged to your room bill — except at Great Keppel Island where many of the activities   are independent of the resort, and for reasons which entirely escaped us, management would not collect for the day-charters but advised guests to carry cash with them.

Cardwell—"best seafood in town"

Prices & Packages

In giving resort and other prices we have relied heavily on their published prices. While we were at resorts we discussed prices with management and tried to get them to project their prices as far into the future as possible. Obviously, though, when you plan your trip it is possible things may have changed. To avoid any confusion over exchange rates, all figures given as $A are in Australian dollars; rates given per person assume twin or double occupancy. (Resorts in the

Barrier Reef area generally impose a hefty surcharge — 50% or more — for single occupancy.) There is no universally agreed high or low "season" in the Barrier Reef. Most resorts increase prices during heavy holiday periods like the Christmas-New Year season, and others have higher rates at other times of the year.

The other side of the coin, however, is that most resorts offer ways to save a few dollars. Almost all — and particularly those in which Australian Airlines or Ansett have an ownership interest — offer package rates combining air fare from Melbourne, Sydney or Brisbane. (At the time of this writing, they had not yet started offering packages via Cairns or Townsville, but we expect they will shortly.) If your plans are such that you will be visiting only one or two islands in the region, and you will be travelling from one of the principal cities, be sure to check with your travel agent, airline or the resort directly for information regarding reduced package rates.

Several resorts offer "standby" rates. These apply if you call within 48 hours of your planned arrival and inquire about available space. It is a clever device of the resorts for filling otherwise empty rooms and will save you at least 15%, and often considerably more, from the cost of accommodations and meals. This is a tariff used by many of the resorts, particularly in the Whitsunday Group.

Hayman Island Resort coffee shop

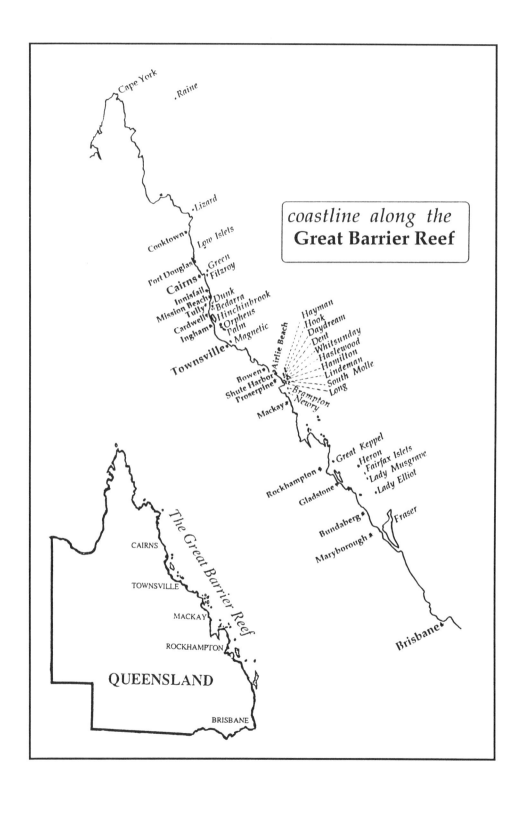

coastline along the
Great Barrier Reef

Islands
of the
Great Barrier Reef

In this chapter, we discuss each of the island resorts of the Great Barrier Reef and a few incident ally interesting islands without resorts. In deciding on the order in which to list them, we had several choices (favorites, north-to-south, south-to-north, price, and so forth) and took the easy way out. They are listed alphabetically for convenient reference, since we have no way of knowing whether you are looking for a single island on which to vacation, a group of islands, the whole string, or even which gateway you might be entering through.

Since the Australians did not have foresight enough to name the islands alphabetically in geographical order, we have prepared the following list to give you several   pieces of information in condensed form. The resort islands are listed running from north to south.   With each, we have indicated the approximate size of the island, number of accommodations, and the price range of accommodations   offered at their resort. Except as indicated to the contrary, note that prices are for full board (three meals) for two people per day so you can compare costs per couple.

Lizard (3.9 sq. miles)	30 rooms	$A460-560
Green(32 acres)	29 units	$A152-192, breakfast and dinner
Fitzroy (510 acres)	5 units	$A168
Dunk (4.7 sq. miles)	140 rooms	$A244-326
Bedarra (250 acres)	32 bungalows (16 each resort)	$A570
Hinchinbrook (231 sq. miles)	30 cabins	$A240-300
Orpheus(8.6 sq. miles)	25 rooms	$A414-454
Magnetic(19 sq. miles)	numerous resorts	$A65-100 or bungalows and small hotels $45 and under, all without meals

The Whitsunday Group

Hayman (1.5 sq. miles)	230 rooms	$A220-450+, without meals
Daydream (26 acres)	78 rooms	$A198-232
South Molle (1.5 sq. miles)	202 rooms	$A230-300
Long (257 acres)		
Whitsunday 100	50 units	$A170
Palm Bay Resort	9 units	$A54-66 without meals
Hamilton (2.4 sq. miles)	400 rooms and growing	$A160-275 without meals
Lindeman (3 sq. miles)	92 rooms	$A168-216

Brampton (195 acres)	100 units	$A244-294
Newry (112 acres)	5 cabins	$A100 (room only $A40)
Great Keppel (5.5 sq. miles)	140 rooms	$A244-266
Heron (42 acres)	90 rooms	$A180-325
Lady Elliot (112 acres)	43 cabin and tent units	$A138-178
Fraser (234 sq. miles)	camping, numerous guest houses, and small hotels	$A20-208, some with meals included

Unfortunately prices do change over time, most often upward. We have done our best to get the most current information at press time. Of course we also cannot anticipate how developments on islands planning additional changes will affect rates.

Bedarra Island

Bedarra Island
•coral viewing
•bushwalks •fishing
•tennis •golf •sailing
•snorkeling •swimming •
•horseback riding

Officially designated Richards Island on navigation charts, Bedarra is located roughly equidistant from Cairns and Townsville. Bedarra, a corruption of an aboriginal word, is three miles from shore and the same distance south of Dunk Island. It is a relatively small island — just over a mile long — yet has eight very nice beaches and is even more beautiful from ashore than when viewed from the sea. It is one of the only islands in the Family Islands group which has abundant water coming from several natural springs. As a result it can comfortably support its tiny resort facilities.

Getting there

Access to Bedarra Island is almost invariably by the *Big Red* launch from nearby Dunk Island (on an as-required basis) or occasionally directly by water taxi from South Mission Beach on the coast just opposite or by launch ($A14 round trip) from Clump Point. Air Queensland flies to Dunk from Townsville ($A154 round trip) daily and from Cairns ($A142 round trip) daily except Thursday.

Except for the northeastern corner which is still private property, this resort island is wholly owned by Australian Airlines (until recently called TransAustralian Airline or TAA) as is neighboring Dunk Island. *The emphasis here is on quiet relaxation.* You can expect to encounter more jungle fowl than people on the paths.

Where to stay & What to do

The resort on Bedarra has been completely rebuilt as two new prize-winning architect designed resorts, *Bedarra Bay* and *Bedarra Hideaway* on opposite sides of the tiny island, each accommodating only thirty-two guests in sixteen luxurious villas. The resorts (both $A285 per person twin share per day includes all meals and drinks, with a large open bar and an open refrigerator chock full of beer, Australian wines, mineral waters and soft drinks in the dining area) are set just off the beach within a thick tropical forest with abundant orchids and other colorful flora. Villas are cleverly integrated into their surroundings such as to be almost invisible from a short distance away. Each is two level, done in Australian timber with polished wood floors, with separate living area and private balcony, generous size bath room with hair dryers and bath robes, ceiling fans and air conditioning, queen size bed, telephones, radio, refrigerator and tea and coffee makers. Furnishings are simple but very elegant.

The centrally located lounge-dining area overlooking the pool and beach has stereo and video systems with a good choice of music or movies. The new resort proudly boasts of its "Cordon Bleu cuisine and food-as-art philosophy."

Guests at Bedarra have access to all of the island with the exception of the small portion of Bedarra which is not part of the resort and is still privately owned by a charming octogenarian artist who is entirely self-sustaining without electricity or regular outside supply. The route for guests between Hideaway and Bedarra Bay is across the island and not along the shoreline; the beaches are not continuous, and it would be impossible to walk along the coast. (One can boat around the island, of course.) Be aware before undertaking the forty-five minute walk through rather dense forest, however, that the path was poorly marked in places. (We found that tying a handkerchief to a branch in one place was a reassuring way of guaranteeing that we would find our way back.) It is a very pleasant jungle trek, passing the lookout just below the island's highest point, 350' Allason Hill.

Bedarra has some of its own recreation facilities and shares others with its sister resort to which there are free launch transfers for registered guests. Catamaran sailing, snorkeling, small motor boats, fresh water swimming pool, paddle skis, cruises to the Outer Barrier Reef, lighted tennis court, hiking, and fishing are the principal activities on this quiet island. Nearby Timana Isle is the home of a well-known Australian artist who produces very distinctive woven tapestries and welcomes visitors from the resort.

One of the most pleasant and delightful things to do here is have the kitchen prepare a picnic hamper for you to take with you to lunch on a private beach; you can request a barbecue, and the staff will fill a cooler with steaks, sausages, chops for you to take on one of the available outboard dinghies. You can sail to one of the secluded beaches, gather some driftwood for a fire on the beach, and cook your own lunch on a grill the staff will give you to take along. Don't forget some of that great Australian beer or wine from the refrigerator on your way to your boat.

All to the plus, however, for those seeking a *hideaway* such as this, there were no evening discos, no crowds, and a beautiful island. The small staff, however, positively bubbles with enthusiasm, and the hideaway idea is so pleasant and romantic that *Bedarra can be the quietest escape among Barrier Reef resorts.* No children or day visitors are allowed. Given its relative accessability by air from Cairns via Dunk, Bedarra may be just what you want for a brief get-away-from-it-all sojourn with next-door bustling activity available at nearby Dunk.

Bedarra Island is just beginning to gain recognition in its own right. Until now it has been a satellite of the Dunk Island resort and has gotten much of its traffic from the small day excursions run from Dunk. Now that the new facility is designed and completed, Australian Airlines is sure to feature it even more. Reservations, already difficult to come by because of the resort's limited capacity, will undoubtedly become a matter of considerable advance planning or last-minute good luck. Fortunately the resort is on the airline computer system, and you can check pretty easily for availability.

Hideaway Resort
via Dunk Island
via Townsville, Qld. 4810
telephone [70] 688 168

Reservations through Australian Airlines or SO/PAC
[800] 551 2012, except California [800] 445 0190

luring fish to the surface

Brampton Island
•coral viewing•national park
•bushwalks•fishing•waterskiing
•anchorage•tennis•golf•sailing
•snorkeling•windsurfing•swimming

Situated just about 20 miles from Mackay, and reached by light aircraft or launch, this popular island is in the Cumberland Islands Group near Whitsunday Passage' southern entrance. Because of its distance from Lindeman, generally considered the southern-most resort among the Whitsunday Group of resorts, Brampton does not get much traffic from charter boats in the Whitsunday Passage; nor does it share much of the resort traffic through Shute Harbor or Hamilton Island.

In earlier days wild horses were bred on this island for use with the Indian army. Some are still found on nearby Carlisle Island, a national park to which you can walk at low tide. Brampton and Carlisle are separated by a narrow channel with coral reefs viewable from glass-bottomed boats at high tide or by wading at low tide. Brampton is a relatively large mountainous island with both open forest and rain-forest. The island boasts white sandy beaches and fringed coral, kangaroos, butterflies and tame rainbow lorikeets (resembling a brightly colored miniature parrot). The top part of the island is a national park forest. Many have described this as the prettiest of the islands in the area.

Getting there

A launch operates from Mackay ($A12 one way) every day at 9:00 a.m. except Tuesday when it departs at 10:00 a.m. for the one hour crossing. Air Queensland has twice daily 20 minute flights from Mackay ($A46 one way) with connections to Brisbane, Rockhampton, Gladstone, Townsville and Cairns. A charming old train takes passengers from jetty to hotel. Day visits to the island are possible; cruises can also be arranged to other islands.

Where to stay

Roylen Cruises, a family business, owned the island since 1962. In 1985 the family sold the entire resort to TransAustralia, now Australian Airlines for $12 million. Company executives indicate that the new project will place an emphasis on couples, but beyond that there are few specifics available yet about future plans. New units have been added; *Carlisle* ($A110 per person, meals included) and *Blue Lagoon* ($A125 per person, with all meals) units have refrigerators and the invariable tea and coffee making equipment. *Brampton Island Resort* has always been considered a not-quite-luxurious, informal resort. It is known chiefly as a place to relax on the beach. The resort's 100 rooms, accommodating a total of 200 guests, are situated in shady settings in a coconut grove originally planted in the last century to provide food for shipwrecked mariners. The fancier holiday units are situated on shady pathways behind the beach. The resort has also added a new swimming pool.

The dining room in the central complex is air conditioned, somewhat unusual amoug Barrier Reef resorts. Buffets and barbecues are featured frequently. There is a nightly party, a resident band at the cabaret, fancy dress nights, sing-along and games nights.

humbug fish

What to do

Island activities include bush walking, good fishing (the chef will cook what you catch), glass bottom boats, water skiing, aquaplane, swimming in the rock pool on the Eastern beach or the saltwater pool on North Beach, tennis and a 5-hole golf course, and the usual resort activities. The resort has a game room, boutique and bank agency.

Brampton historically seemed to charge for everything: an oyster bucket rented for fifty cents. Yet they seem to have a clientele of people who come back year after year; obviously returning guests come for the beautiful beaches and relaxed atmosphere, and by now they have learned to bring their own oyster buckets. What Australian Airlines will finally do with this island in the future is still unknown; since things have been getting a little frayed around the edges, however, it's possible that the change will do the old place lots of good.

Brampton Island
P.O. Box 169
Mackay, Qld. 4740
telephone[79] 572 595

Reservations through McLeans Roylen Cruises,
River Street Mackay, Qld. 4740; telephone [79] 572 595 or 421 333, or through Australian Airlines

Daydream Island

Daydream Island
•coral viewing•national park
•bushwalks•fishing•waterskiing
•scuba diving•tennis•sailing
•snorkeling•windsurfing•swimming

The brochure says it:*"Daydream is a small tropical island — and the whole island is a resort — not just a resort on an island."* Part of the Whitsunday Island group and known on the navigation charts as West Molle Island, Daydream was named after a cruising yacht well known in the area in the 1930's. It is indeed a very small lush twenty-seven acre tropical island — in fact the smallest of the settled islands in the area — situated about two miles east of Shute Harbor with in the Whitsunday Passage. Near the resort, the beaches are rocky, but at the north end of the island there is a superb white coral sand beach. Parts of the island are rain forest with very rich areas of beautiful vegetation.

Getting there

Reached by launch from Shute Harbor (20 mins, $A20 round trip) which departs at 9:00 a.m. and 5:00 p.m. daily or by boat from Hamilton Island ($A40) which connects with most flights, the *Daydream Island Resort* will also arrange bus pick-up at Proserpine airport ($A40 round trip includes the launch). On the way from Shute Harbor, you get a delightful tour of Whitsunday Passage, truly one of the most beautiful waterways in the world. Daydream provides very limited anchorage for visiting yachts on the back, or eastern side. There are day trips available to Daydream which include barbecue lunch around the pool and all beach activities (water skiing extra).

Where to stay

Daydream was one of the first coral islands in this area to be developed for tourism. It is visited mainly by Australians and has not become very well known in the American market (so advises affable assistant manager Gail Witcher who has been in Australia 16 years but still has a very detectable trace of Minnesota in her speech). Developed by Cobb & Co. (a Queensland-based bus company), the resort was purchased by Ansett Airlines when they bought Hayman and was then demolished in 1952. Gold Coast entrepreneur Bernie Elsey purchased the lease from Ansett and developed the island for tourism in 1968. The resort was totally flattened by hurricane Ada in 1970 but was rebuilt with a fairly impressive and sturdy complex of motel-type units.

The hotel sits at the southern end of the island. It consists of two-story modern tropical wood frame buildings containing 96 units with each room facing the beach to the front and with a view of Whitsunday passage from back windows; you are certainly aware of the fact that you're on an island here. There are three styles of accommodations, all with private bath, air-conditioning and ceiling fans, iron and ironing board, refrigerators, tea and coffee maker, direct dial telephones, radio and color television. Use of all island water facilities is included in the room rates without extra charge except for water skiing and scuba diving.

Poolside Suites ($A99 per person per day, all meals included) are downstairs around the large swimming pool. *Daydreamer Suites* ($A105) upstairs have even better views of the Whitsunday Passage. The six *VIP Suites* and the more elegant *Sunlover Lodge* (both $A116) are larger and have full bath rather than shower and nicer amenities. Like several other Whitsunday area resorts, Daydream offers a stand-by rate ($A59) for people calling within 24 hours of their arrival and accepting accommodation on an as-available basis.

The resort has just undergone refurbishing and remodelling. It has a very comfortable and pleasantly appointed Polynesian-decor restaurant and a cavernous bar lounge (with nightly live entertainment) for dancing, cabaret, disco, fancy dress nights, "horse racing night", talent quests, and other theme nights. There is a small downstairs *Down Under Bar*, open until late at night, where new guests also are met by the management and oriented to the resort. Buffet breakfast, poolside barbecues for lunch, served four course dinners with a small but adequate and very moderately priced wine list. The resort has a tropical island seafood smorgasbord twice a week. There is also a small coffee shop.

What to do

Activities include a large free-form swimming pool with a bar in the center, scuba instruction (including a free introductory lesson in the pool and intermediate training allowing you to dive with an instructor or dive master), badminton, cruises to other islands and the outer reef, fishing, a good all weather tennis court, volley ball, paddle skis, snorkeling, coral viewing from a private barge, six-person outrigger canoe, boom netting, volley ball, table tennis, pool tables, wind surfing, spa and sauna. You can walk or ride the motorboat to Sunlovers Beach, the beautiful small secluded beach area for sunbathing and snorkeling at the north end of the island. There are also beautiful walks through the tropical forest on the island. The resort also has movies and video games. There is a small well stocked store (which will take virtually any credit card *except* Master Charge). There are coin laundry facilities.

As with most Whitsunday Group resorts, there are many opportunities to visit the other resorts in the immediate vicinity — particularly South Molle, and the proximity of Shute Harbor makes it fairly easy to traverse back and forth. This also allows you to take advantage of some of the day charters, such as reef excursions and fishing trips, based at nearby resorts.

Daydream Island is what would have to be called a sleeper. Management is cordial, personable, and highly motivated to see that every guest has a good time. People are addressed by name by the staff whenever possible, and every effort is made to avoid the routine or institutional approach to resort life. It is a quiet resort and a relaxing island. It that's what you're in the mood for, this is one of those small, less expensive resorts that might well be the absolutely perfect base of operation for a great vacation.

Daydream Island Resort
Daydream Island via Shute Harbor
Qld. 4800
[79] 469 200; telex 48519

Reservations through Daydream Island

strolling peacock

Dent Island
•no resort
•coral arts business

In the Whitsunday area, this long narrow island west of Hamilton Island has *no resort*. The manned lighthouse on the island was established in 1874. Septuagenarians Lene and Bill Wallace, retired Americans who have occupied the island for years, have established a coral arts business adjacent to the sandy beach just across from the Hamilton Island marina (day trip from Hamilton $A8). Many people sail by and stop to see their coral art work and relax on the island. The buildings are situated in a palm grove where one finds many strolling peacocks. The yacht anchorage, however, is poor, and the approach is easier on a small power boat.

Dunk Island

Dunk Island

*•coral viewing•national park
• buskwalks•fishing•waterskiing
•anchorage•tennis•golf•sailing
•snorkeling•windsurfing
•swimming•horseback riding*

This large tropical island is located about 100 miles south of Cairns, about the same distance north of Townsville, and around two miles off the coast, opposite and within sight of the small town of Mission Beach. In the other direction, it is 15 miles from the Great Barrier Reef. Dunk, with its lush jungle and tropical rain forest, its fascinating giant butterflies, abundant beautiful tropical birds — including the exotic large white sulphur-crested cockatoo, and long palm-bordered sand beaches may well have the *best natural attributes* of all of the Barrier Reef resorts.

In 1896 Townsville journalist E.J. Banfield took a lease on the island and later was granted ownership of an agricultural homestead on which he and his wife lived until his death twenty years later after gaining recognition as the author of several books on the joys of living as a beachcomber and lover of nature. The ownership of Dunk passed to others who later started to develop it seriously for tourism, ultimately carving an airstrip across the peninsula and building accommodations.

Dunk Island is one of Queensland's more luxurious and sophisticated island resorts. It is the main island of the Family Group, having twelve islands in all, with Bedarra Island the other developed resort in the group.

Much of the island is rain forest with dozens of varieties of tropical birds visible along the track leading to the summit of Mount Koo-ta-loo. Dunk beaches feature unusually fine sand on the northern side of island, which is quite uncommon on barrier reef islands. Much of Dunk Island — particularly the rain forest — is protected national park.

The island is known for its magnificent (if somewhat elusive) giant butterflies, particularly the giant blue *Ulysses butterfly* (whose four to six inch wing spread has been exaggerated in fable — and tourism literature — to be twelve inches). Don't be disappointed if you only see smaller blue butterflies. Climb to the top of *Koo-ta-loo* along the fairly easy path (about two hours up and back), and you're almost certain to see one or another impressively large butterfly — quite possibly the lovely *Cairns Green Birdwing* — among the trees of the rain forest. (If you do take this beautiful walk, remember that you are in the tropics where both temperature and humidity are higher than they feel; because there are no facilities along the way, *take along some fruit or something to drink so you don't become dehydrated.*)

Getting there

Dunk is easily reached by air from Cairns by Air Queensland (just over $A50 each way for the forty-five minute trip) which operates several daily flights using DeHavilland Twin Otters. Air Queensland also has daily flights from Townsville using the same aircraft for about the same price. If you can get to Mission Beach midway between Cairns and Townsville (for example, by the bus service which runs once or twice a day on the coast highway) there are several water taxi companies which can take you to Dunk ($A27 for 1-5 persons). There are two launches ($A12 round trip) leaving from nearby Clump Point about six miles from Dunk by water. Reaching Dunk by way of the bus is more complex than flying, however, since it requires fairly close scheduling, a two hour bus ride from Townsville or Cairns to Tully (about $A6), taxi from Tully to Clump Point and then the forty-five minute launch to Dunk.

Where to stay & What to do

The resort is owned by Australian Airlines (formerly TAA), the government-owned carrier, which makes every effort to run a sophisticated efficient operation. The staff greets guests on arrival at the island's airstrip with a complimentary glass of champagne and orange juice. Brief registration formalities are taken care of right at the terminal. Guests are greeted by name as they present their vouchers and have their names checked off the arrival list and then are efficiently transported directly to their rooms aboard a van or small bus. Room assignments have been completed in advance so there is no delay in getting to your room and immediately into the spirit of the island. Luggage is brought along shortly after by one of the porters (they're the ones wearing the shirt labeled *porter* — and they don't stand by hoping for a gratuity.)

Management has spent more than $2.3 million on its Great Barrier Reef Hotel, with 140 well designed top-class units accommodating up to 320 guests. There are three distinct types of accommodations. *Banfield units* ($A122 per person, double occupancy, including all meals) are two-story buildings set back in tropical surroundings. *Cabana Suites* ($A135) are scattered around the central complex in a tropical garden setting. *Beachfront Cabanas* ($A163) are just off the beach, are air conditioned, and offer considerably more privacy. All of these prices include virtually all activities and facilities, except for those requiring fuel such as power boats.

All of the rooms show attention to architectural and interior decorating detail. In the Cabana Suites, an entire wall is glass with a large sliding door to the terrace. The ceilings are very high (perhaps sixteen feet), and the space is ample. Open the front glass door and back door, keeping the screens closed, and the overhead circulating fan facilitates pleasant circulation of the tropical breezes. Decor is simple, with emphasis on light colors, including the floor tile and light woven mat floor cover, creating a pleasantly sophisticated clean tropical effect. The bathroom facilities are modest but quite satisfactory.

Twice-a-day housemaid service is efficient and always a welcome plus at any resort, but as with a few other Barrier Reef resorts you have to plead for extra towels to take to beach or pool. Go to the resort laundry, located behind the guest laundry facilities, and ask the staff for a couple of towels which they will be delighted to furnish. The drinks man restocks your room refrigerator daily and will take orders for extra sodas or specific wines from the resort's ample wine list for your room.

Life at Dunk is very informal for a sophisticated resort. Dress up for dinner means putting on a shirt with a collar and, if shorts are worn, long socks. The large dining pavilion is open-air and nicely laid out. Light music — one day pop classics, another day "golden oldies", but neither obnoxious nor elevator music — is piped in during breakfast and lunch, and a pianist plays light classics during dinner.

Buffet breakfast is an exceptionally nice array of fresh fruits, cereals, juices, and a hot table with a broad selection from eggs to steak to spaghetti. Lunch is again a buffet — we felt it was the very best luncheon buffet among Barrier Reef resorts — and is generally the best meal of the day at Dunk. The buffet table was perfect for the tropics: fresh cold giant prawns, fish salads, a broad selection of cold meats and salads, a hot table with fresh reef fish, (overly) breaded scallops and shrimps, quiche, stir fried vegetables, and meats. There was also   a cheese board and large selection of fresh fruits. A drinks waiter will take your order, serving beer, wines or whatever.

During our stay dinner, served à la carte with a choice of three main courses (remember Australia calls the preliminary course the entrée), was somewhat uneven. Perhaps we were more critical of Dunk than other resorts because the dining room came so highly advertised, or perhaps the particular kitchen staff that month wasn't operating at peak performance. Regrettably our dinners were not as the travel promotion literature had predicted. The first evening, the appetizer course of king prawns served with a very light cocktail sauce was absolutely delightful — as good as the TV commercials for Australian tourism suggest. On the other hand, the main courses generally were a little disappointing.

Coq au vin (here cooked with red wine, bacon and mushroom sauce) tasted too much of canned mushroom sauce and the chicken was less than perfect. Beef Wellington seemed at tad contrived; we felt that a simple steak would have been preferable to their presentation. The coral trout teriyaki — a "fillet of coral trout marinated in soy sauce, orange juice, ginger and spring onions, and grilled" — tasted like it was marinated only in soy sauce and grilled...and grilled...and grilled! We   began to wonder if, because the resort is owned by an airline, the kitchen felt the need to serve airline food at least once a day.

There are some very distinct pluses in the dining room in the evening, The dining pavilion itself is a very attractive, inviting large open struc- ture, well appointed and very pleasantly staffed. The service is pleasant and attentive. The atmosphere is very congenial and provides ample opportunities for visiting with the other guests of the resort. While by no means overly formal, there is a pleasant sophistication to the operation.

The cheese board — set up in the middle of the dining room on a serve-yourself basis — was simple but excellent. The wine list is some- thing of which the resort can well be proud. They have fairly priced the local wines and offer a broad selection. Other visitors have had very pleasant things to say about Dunk's cuisine. In all likelihood the fine reputation it has in the region was earned and deserved. We certainly wouldn't discourage anyone from visiting this resort just because our dinners   fell a bit short of the standards described in their brochure.

Indeed one regular Dunk dining event stands out as a stellar food attraction of the entire region. Friday evening the resort features its *seafood smorgasbord* with fresh prawns, superb Queensland mud crabs (which, we reported earlier, are quite similar to San Francisco dungenous crab), Moreton Bay bugs (those delicious baby lobsters we also mentioned earlier), sand crabs, abalone, smoked eel, reef fish and oysters, to which they add whole roast suckling pig, turkey, ham and assorted salads. The selection is excellent, definitely ample, and beautifully laid out. The kitchen staff is available at the buffet table to explain the various selections and to see that the platters are kept heaping full. It's easy to understand why many visitors bring their cameras to this affair.

For those wishing a lighter a la carte dinner, *Banfield's Restaurant* is available. Meals here are separately charged, however.

A few steps opposite the dining pavilion, the open two-story high entertainment complex is a large pleasant space with comfortable and attractive seating arrangements. The tropical island style building is done in regional woods with attractive colorful fabrics. The main bar as well as the dance floor are situated here, and the atmosphere — both day and evening, overlooking the swimming pool and the bay beyond, is delightful and relaxing. After dinner there is live entertainment and the resident dance band (of course calling themselves *Papillon*, after the island's abundant supply of butterflies) plays every night. Generally the music is a mix of sixties and seventies U.S. pop rock. On Saturday they have western night! There is a television lounge where a recent release afternoon movie is shown daily and Jane Fonda videotape exercise programs are run once or twice a day. For the very hungry, there is a coffee shop. There is also a hair dressing salon, baby sitting service (at normal rates other than during dinner, when they will care for your child over three for free while you dine), conference facilities for 80, telex, and two STD pay phones — the only telephones available to resort guests (meaning occasional lines in the evening) — located outside the reception office.

The resort has laid out three or four pleasant walks to and around various parts of the island. These graded walks are charted on a map provided by the resort. Pay attention to their time estimates; it takes longer to walk about on this island than you might expect, and the forest could prove very mystifying and even a bit frightening if you are lost there at dusk. The stroll to the southern coast Coconut Beach is about two hour round trip. Along the way you get a splendid view of islands within 5 miles. There are daily horseback riding excursions as well.

Bedarra, 3 miles away, is separately operated as a very exclusive resort by Australian Airlines. The *Big Red* powerboat makes the trip as needed to transport Bedarra guests who fly into Dunk as well as occasionally to transport Bedarra guests to participate in activities on Dunk. **Timana Island,** to west of Bedarra, can technically be reached on foot at low tide (but a boat is a safer idea) from the mangrove flats at the southern end of the Dunk Island runway and is the home of a well known Australian tapestry artist.

Fifty-minute sea plane trips to the Outer Barrier Reef ($A35) take five people for a breathtaking view of the large expanse of reef. This type of excursion may be the only way to appreciate the reef in broad perspective, even though it truly still only displays a relatively small portion of the grandeur of this fantastic natural structure. Day-long launch trips on the ten passenger *Avenger* ($A60, including lunch, but drinks a small charge extra) or *Gamefisher* ($A70) to the Outer Barrier Reef (weather and tides permitting, as with so many activities involving the Outer Reef) give you a chance to snorkel and fish on the   very edge of the sea protected by the massive reef.

There is a pretty golf course (6-hole, except on Sunday when they commandeer one of the holes for Lord Montague Dunk Ground where they hold a cricket match —"Dunk's Dozen" versus "Australia"), archery range behind the tennis courts, horse riding on trails through the forest ($A8), catamarans and wind surfers, water skiing (a tad expensive at $A5 per run or $30 for half hour), clay pigeon shooting, badminton court, volleyball, pool table, ping pong, and tennis courts with a strange simulated grass/carpet surface (called *Super Grasse*) which collects blown sand, making it most interesting to try to predict the bounce. Incidentally, the resort provides tennis rackets and balls and golf clubs and carts without charge.

There are limited laundry facilities — four washing machines, dryers, irons and boards — available for resort guests without charge — and they even give you laundry soap. The machines are quite busy during the daytime, but since they are available twenty-four hours, you might consider using them later in the evening or before an early game of tennis before breakfast.

Australian Airlines continues what, according to one
writer, has become a Dunk
tradition — "that of changing
managers every few days,
weeks, or months. In less
than fifteen years there have
been well over fifty managers." If there is any short-
coming at Dunk Island it is a
perceptible lack of imagination on the part of management. For example, the resort manager and most of the
executive staff left the manager's weekly welcoming
party early when we were

beach on Dunk Island

there and were not present to greet guests who accepted the resort's
invitation for cocktails. As another instance, no one at the reception
desk could even begin to suggest how to go about planning direct
transportation to Hinchinbrook resort, situated on a massive island
visible from Dunk, because evidently none of the people working behind
the desk had ever visited Hinchinbrook. You should also be aware that,
since reception is open only at 9:00 a.m.(and not a minute earlier, and
doors are locked until then), you must be sure to make appropriate
arrangements if you have an early departure by water taxi, since all
check-out activity — including baggage pick-up and transport — at this
sizeable resort is geared around scheduled departures by air.

Dunk offers you every opportunity for a very action filled holiday in a
lovely environment at a generally very efficiently operated resort. It
offers as much in the way of ocean-centered activity as any other resort.
Dunk is very popular with families (that means lots of little kids, if that's
important to you) and is a great place for an easy holiday, particularly if
accessability from Cairns is important in your planning.

Dunk Island Resort
Dunk Island via Townsville, Qld. 4810
[70] 688 199

Reservations through Australian Airlines

on Dunk Island

Fairfax Island
•*no resort*
•*coral cays*
•*no tourist facilities*

You may come across reference to Fairfax in literature about the Great Barrier Reef. It actually consists of two coral cays in the Bunker Group south of Heron Island and below the Tropic of Capricorn. Vegetation on the windward cay was destroyed by practice bombing during World War II representing a tragic, irreparable loss. There are *no resort or tourist facilities* on these cays.

Fitzzoy Island

Fitzroy Island
•coral viewing
•bushwalks •fishing
•snorkeling •swimming

This continental island in the Coral Sea, only 14 miles from Cairns and 8 miles from the Outer Barrier Reef, is fringed with beaches that ring like crystal when you walk on the heavy coral gravel which has been washed up over the sand. A small dense tropical rain forest includes eucalyptus, streams, waterfalls, wild orchids, butterflies. This is an unspoiled island with beautiful coral flats, a   good deep anchorage, and ample fresh water.

There is no evidence that any aboriginal tribe inhabited Fitzroy, althoughit was used as a hunting ground. There is some chance that early Chinese, Japanese, and natives from New Guinea visited the island — and others off North   Queensland — but left no modern day discernible traces. The first sighting of Fitzroy Island by a European was by Captain Cook on June 10, 1770. He named the island in honor of the Duke of Grafton, a prominent politician and illegitimate son of Charles II. Two days later, Cook's ship, the *Endeavor*, ran aground on the reef.

The abundance of fresh water made the island very attractive to subsequent nautical visitors. During the late nineteenth century there was a large Chinese migration to north Australia. Partly due to European prejudices and partly to the threat of small pox from China, Fitzroy was in 1877 made a quarantine station for Chinese immigrants who were required to remain there for sixteen days to test for signs of ill health. Evidently these quarantine periods were extended so long as officials could detect the slightest signs of ill health, with the result that many Chinese did not survive the quarantine and are buried on the island.

Getting there

Access to Fitzroy Island is by *M.V. Fitzroy Flyer,* a high speed (28 knot) catamaran which carries 172 passengers,   departing Fitzroy Marina on the

Esplanade in Cairns daily at 9:00 a.m. for the 40 minute trip. The "two island" trip ($27 round trip — $20 off season — plus $13 if you want the buffet lunch and glass bottom boat trip on Fitzroy) includes an afternoon stop at Green Island. The lunch at Fitzroy resort is $A10 and can be purchased after arrival. There is also an optional trip to the Outer Reef in addition to Green and Fitzroy which takes one hour each way from the islands but is very weather sensitive. Friday and Saturday nights the *Fitzroy Flyer* operates special schedules returning to the mainland about midnight to allow day visitors to attend the resort's weekend entertainments. On Wednesday nights the island's stores are ferried over, so the resort operates a "booze cruise" evening round trip.

Where to stay & What to do

The resort currently has accommodations for a maximum of 30 overnight guests ($A84 per person per day with all meals; children $A39.50) in five self-contained villas (up to 6 people accommodated in each) just off the beach. We were told that the local government authorities plan to allow expansion of the island's facilities in the next few years, in part to alleviate the increasing congestion on nearby Green Island.

Units are very clean but relatively spartan. They have a double bed, single bunk, and a back room, really an enclosed porch, with a double bunk. Cabins have private bath, color television, radio, ceiling fan, large patio, unstocked refrigerator and kitchen sink but no serious cooking capability beyond a toaster. Laundry facilities are available.

The quite pleasant open central complex has restaurant and bar, dive shop and souvenir stand. There is a fast-food kiosk, selling fish and chips, huge hot dogs, and the like, with a good selection of soft drinks. Friday and Saturday nights the resort features professional entertainment.

Lunch is a fixed price ($A10) affair. On our first visit it was a beautiful cold smorgasbord spread. Our favorites were the cold roast chicken and cold steamed baramundi served with a slice of pineapple and a traditional selection of sauces at the end of the buffet. The choice of cold cuts and salads was quite satisfactory. Fresh cold vegetables and fruit set off the table nicely. By our second visit, the smorgasbord had been abandoned in favor of a barbecue which offered a selection of meats done on the grill while you wait and was quite nice. There was a pleasant selection of salads and other accompaniments.

Feel free to take your plate outside and sit on the terrace overlooking the bay for the best table in town . The bar stocks at quite moderate prices a rather good selection of Australian wines and several beers which adds up to a very nice luncheon.

You can view the coral from a glass-bottom boat for an hour each day at 11:00 a.m.; explore the island using one of the well marked walking tracks through the rain forrest, to the light house or the butterfly glen. There is a new semi-submersible, one of the new breed of motorized barges with a large underwater bubble, this one seating about 25 people ($A10) for a lovely cruise around the island's reef. Underwater the bay contains 300 varieties of live coral. Swarming shoals of small fish have been tamed by twice daily tropical fish feeding from the jetty. The resort also has paddle skiing (glass panel skis available), fishing, canoeing, water bikes — "even a nudey beach" says the brochure. Lie on the beach, snorkel or just relax in a paddle boat. There is no swimming pool, however.

In 1984 the government established a breeding station for the giant sea clams which have become nearly extinct in the vicinity because of over-fishing by Taiwanese poachers who find a large market in China where the clams are considered to possess aphrodisiac properties. Regrettably the operators charge to view the rather nondescript clam facility which consists of a few large concrete vats; you can just as well peek over the fence and eavesdrop. (According to a marine biologist who works there, it takes about 15 months to raise a clam large enough to be sold commercially or deposited on the reef, ultimately to grow to 10 kilo grams of bivalve or larger).

We enjoyed our brief sojourns to Fitzroy. It is an easy and pleasant day trip from Cairns, and the Flyer makes a nice introduction to the Barrier Reef world if you enter through that Gateway and have time to spare. *Fitzroy could also offer a very quiet, very secluded resort vacation,* but the quietude and limited activity schedule would suggest only a brief holiday unless total relaxation is your goal.

Fitzroy Island
P.O. Box 2120
Cairns, Qld. 4870
telephone[70] 557 118

Reservations through Fitzroy Island,
c/o Tourist Booking Office,
Marlin Parade,
Cairns, Qld. 4870;
telephone [70] 515 477

a rain forest

Fraser Island
•*bushwalks*
•*fishing*
•*snorkeling*
•*swimming*
•*camping*

This is the largest sandy island in the world and is located approximately 150 miles north-east of Brisbane. The sand which makes up the island is not even from the region, but instead the sea has carried it from the south until it piled up against undersea obstacles. The dense plant life which has developed prevents the giant island from being washed away. A great deal of political controversy surrounded the island during the 1970s when Australia's strong conservationist movement succeeded in having the federal government declare a ban on timber and sand mining operations on Fraser.

Fraser Island is not truly part of the Great Barrier Reef region being well south of the southern extent of the reef itself. It is geographically close, however, and advertises in many of the same publications that promote Barrier Reef holidays. If you are travelling north from Brisbane, it could be along the way.

Here you find wilderness, freshwater lakes, rocky headlands and forests. Part of the island is a national   park. Because of its sub-tropical location, Fraser combines tropical and temperate with birds and fish of both climates. There are dense rain forests with abundant wildlife. The most prominent features of the island are *towering sand dunes* as high as 750 feet above sea level, *Woongoolbver Creek* with its sandy bottom and canopy of palms, ferns and vines, and *Lake Wabby* (its deepest lake) and numerous other lakes. Fraser is advertised as a geologist's fantasy, a naturalist's workshop and in parts, a scenic imperative and it boasts a coastline of almost 200 miles.

It is hard to explore this island, however. The terrain is a series of sharp defined sand dunes which has been characterized as an endless repetition of ridges. These peaks are very close together, so one would constantly be climbing and descending sand hills. Add to this the thickness of the vegetation, and you have a real wilderness adventure. The island is criss-crossed with forestry tracks suitable for four-wheel-drive vehicles, but at the very least these are a real navigational challenge. Should you desire to undertake this test, you must obtain a permit to leave the shore areas. Consult the Duty Ranger on the island or the National Parks and Wildlife Service in Brisbane for visiting permits and the District Forester in Maryborough for driving permits.

Getting there

Fraser Island is reached by air from Brisbane, Maryborough or Hervey Bay via Sunstate Airlines. Charter flights are available ($100/hour for 5-seat aircraft and $A180/hour for 9-seat) from Whittakers Air Services in Maryborough [telephone (071) 22 2255]. There is also car ferry service from either Inskip Point on the mainland to Hook Point (daily between 6:30 a.m. and 4:00 p.m., ten minute trip, $A30-32 per vehicle) or Bullock Point on the island; or Urangan on the coast to Moon Point or Urang Creek; or River Heads to Deep Creek. The barge landing is 67 miles from Orchid Beach.

Where to stay & What to do

Orchid Beach Island Village ($A94-104 per person, meals included [telephone (07) 283 822; telex 49683]), overlooking Marloo Bay, is a polynesian-style resort with twenty-five cabins with shower and fan, licensed dining room, pool, tennis court, fishing, water skiing, and evening entertainment.

At Happy Valley, about 30 miles north of Inskip Point, *Beacon Lodge Holiday Flats* [telephone Happy Valley 4U] has a self-contained flat which will accommodate six persons ($A22/day for two persons; $A130/week). *Boom Crest* [telephone (071) 82 2522)] has two flats for 1-6 persons ($A28/day; $A160 180/week, linen rental extra). *Elanora* [telephone Happy Valley 1] also has two flats for 1-6 persons ($A26-40/day; $A150-180/week, linen rental extra). *Fraser Lodge* and *Fraser Unit* [telephone Happy Valley 6k] each have one flat accommodating 8 ($A26-30/day; $A130-180/week, linen extra). *Fraser Sands* has two flats accommodating six persons ($A24-30/day; $A10-160/week), *Murava House* [telephone (071) 82 3447] has one flat for six persons ($A24-30/day; $A150-180/week).

Eurong Beach Resort [telephone Ungowa 7U] offers a choice between the resort and lodge style accommodations. There are 35 units accommodating up to 8 persons, some with fans, radio, coffee and tea makers, refrigerators and cooking facilities   ($A35 per day per person with all meals; $A135-185/week for 1-8 persons without meals.) There are *general stores* at Eurong Beach Tourist Resort and Happy Valley. There is a *National Fitness Camp* at Dilli Village, 5 miles south of Eurong.

Sunrover Rentals offer self-drive packages which include the cost of a four-wheel drive vehicle and camping gear ($A152 per day for up to four people) or a beach hut ($A168 per day for up to four people). These include the round trip ferry travel, access permits on the island,   fishing gear, and vehicle service in the event of a breakdown.

There are cruise tours available to Fraser on the Fraser Princess and M.V. Philanderer out of Urangan. For further information contact:

Queensland Tourist and Travel Corp.,
3550 Wilshire Boulevard
Los Angeles, California   90010;

telephone [213] 381-3062

Hervey Bay Town Council
corner Bideford and Campbell Streets,
Torquay, Qld. 4657;

telephone [071] 28 2855.

on Great Keppel

Great Keppel Island

•coral viewing •national park
•bushwalks •fishing •waterskiing
•anchorage •tennis •sailing
•snorkeling •windsurfing
•swimming •camping

"The perfect place for a tropical suntan, making friends and dancing the night away," says one Aussie tourist bureau promotion piece. Great Keppel Island lies just inside the Tropic of Capricorn, 30 to 35 miles northeast of Rockhampton, eight miles off the coast. It was also the largest of the group of Barrier Reef islands named by Captain Cook. Once a sheep station, the old homestead is intact on the mountain. There are also private homes on the island near the resort. It is one of the larger resort islands and is gifted with *seventeen sandy white beaches* covering 17 miles. This island claims to have more sunshine than any other area off the East Coast of Australia. It is 24 miles from the nearest point on the outer Great Barrier Reef.

Getting there

Great Keppel is reached by most resort guests by means of the 15 to 20 minute flight from Rockhampton on Sunstate Airlines 20-passenger DeHavilland Twin Otter ($A75.40 round trip; price included in packages). It is a beautiful short flight, giving you a chance to see the coastal region where some of Australia's best beef is raised, the Fitzroy river, pineapple plantations, some mangrove swamps, and the coastal beach towns of Rosslyn Bay and Yeppoon. Although there is a daily launch ($A14 round trip) — and talk of a four-day-a-week hydrofoil which we never saw ($A18 round trip) — from Rosslyn Bay Boat Harbor via Yeppoon approximately 43 miles north of Rockhampton, getting from "Rocky" airport to the wharf may prove tricky so most visitors from outside of North Queensland arrive by air.

There is a somewhat open but adequate anchorage, and there are many nearby islands which make the idea of chartering a boat for a few days to see Great Keppel and its surroundings a pleasant prospect for qualified sailors. You can check local listings, which you can pick up at the Rockhampton airport, for boat and yacht rental agencies.

Where to stay

Much of Great Keppel is national park. Some small portions are privately owned fee interests where there are private residences. The balance of the island, including the entire resort, is located on an old grazing leasehold which was purchased outright in the mid-1970's by Australian Airlines (formerly TransAustralia Airlines or TAA), which also owns and operates Brampton, Dunk and Bedarra Island resorts several hundred miles to the north. *Great Keppel Resort* located at Fishermans' Beach has 160 rather undistinguished motel type units with accommodations for over 400 guests.

The resort has 160 rooms. Two types of *Garden bungalows* ($A122 per person per day, double occupancy, including all meals) are available, some of which are older single-story standard class while others are smaller but newer garden units in a large two story L-shaped blockhouse facing the tennis courts (same prices). *Beachfront units* ($A133 per person per day) are the same as the smaller garden rooms but are in a blockhouse facing the water. There were formerly several units described as "Deluxe" which are considerably larger than the other beachfront rooms. The recent expansion program, however, has cut off the beach view from these rooms, so they have been down-classified and will rent as beachfront without the view. These in fact are probably the superior accommodations in the resort, with small tub and shower as well as balconies or verandas, but evidently will be issued out by the computer at random in the beachfront category. There are two *super-deluxe suites* (approximately $A300 per day) but these are not in the reservations computer and are held principally for visiting VIPs.

Speaking of the computer, the whole operation at Great Keppel is apparently conducted out of Australian Airlines' central offices connected electronically with the resort. As a result the resort cannot give credits or make financial adjustments, and any refunds must come out of Brisbane.

The resort's rooms need refurbishing and remodelling, but regrettably the recent $A3 million expansion program evidently did not budget for that. Units have chartreuse chenille bedspreads and industrial indoor-outdoor carpeting. The walls in the single-story bungalow units are insufficiently adorned painted clapboard, and the balance of the rooms are painted cinderblock with gunnite ceilings. Facilities include private shower and toilet in plain utilitarian bathrooms, ceiling fan, unstocked refrigerator, tea and coffee making facilities. There are no dressers or proper vanities. Lighting is poor.

Ventilation in the older regular units is primitive and poor. The overhead fan circulates the air, but there are insufficient windows and doors for cross- ventilation, so the rooms remain quite warm — five to ten degrees warmer, in fact, than the outside tropical world. The beachfront and newer garden units are considerably smaller than the "family" apartments and are situated in ranks of two story block houses, but it is at least possible to open the entrance door at one end and sliding glass doors at the other to catch any breezes.

Meals are served in the *Admiral Keppel Dining Room.* Great Keppel Island was named after this First Lord of the Admiralty by Captain Cook. We are told that the Admiral never set foot on this island and, never having married, left no descendants. This is all to the good, for it spares his heirs the embarrassment which would be caused them by having their name identified with this poor excuse for a dining room. It was all right that the resort tried to imitate the interior of an old sailing ship — they have hooked the ceiling lanterns up so they cutely sway uniformly from side to side through dinner, (but, thank goodness, not breakfast and lunch as well) — but the industrial white plastic ceiling quickly breaks the spell, and the well worn indoor-outdoor carpet with random plank wood stenciled on it is too much. And we truly doubt that any ship's galley was ever crowded with formica tables, and stackable chairs as you had in your high school cafeteria.

We were promised by the promotional literature that breakfasts offered unlimited fruit juice, eggs, bacon, sausages, fruit, tea or coffee. This is true as far as it goes, but what it really describes is an unattractive buffet where no one pays much attention to the appearance of the food which has been dumped unceremoniously on serving platters. The hot table is adequate, but for an island resort the cold fruit selection is not.

Lunch promised *"a mountainous smorgasbord of hot & cold dishes,"* seafood, fruit, salads, cold meats. Translated this became a few cold cuts — no cold fish and no cheeses, a very small selection of salad materials, and mediocre hot foods. Luncheon beverages are also entirely self-service.

Dinner was of the same quality. The soup course —seafood chowder, oxtail, tomato — with only one type (no choices) each evening is followed by one entrée (again no choices) such as overly breaded frozen prawns or, another night, an avocado vinaigrette which was actually rather good. The main courses were quite uneven. One evening the fish was fresh and flavorful; the next it was bland and drowned in a thick commercial sauce. The chicken orientale (soy sauce, on a bed of rice) was quite fine, but the beef iwasaki (soy sauce, pineapple and ginger) was poor. Desserts were generally unimaginative, although to be fair the apple pie when offered was very enjoyable, and the pleasant staff told us we could always just request plain ice cream, which was fairly good. A very small thoroughly uninspired but inexpensive wine list, with the bulk of the offerings in the $A12-16 range, provided appropriate accompaniment to the food.

Friday is "Island Night":: a buffet "under the stars" including seafood, cold cuts, salads, fruits and cheeses." Sound familiar — larger lunch plus fish? Right, but scratch dessert — not offered with this particular dinner. The addition of Moreton Bay bugs (those exquisite midget lobsters they get in Queensland) was nice, and the very nice woman serving them — these they don't let you help yourself to — gave us each *one* , which is like being given one big prawn. The chilled mud crab, another Queensland specialty, was left on a platter so guests could serve themselves a more generous portion.

To compound matters, the Friday buffet dinner is served around the rectangular swimming pool outside the dining room and is very poorly organized so that it can only be approached on one side of the tables. Moreover there is only one platter of each item. The result is that you have to be prepared for a very long line until just before dinner ends at 8:00. On balance, we would have to say this was about the least impressive buffet we found anywhere among Barrier Reef resorts.

For the collegiate or superannuated beer bust set there are programmed night time activities generally beginning by 10:30 p.m. and going on until every one reaches exhaustion. Six nights a week the resident rock group livens up the *Wreck Bar* until approximately 2:00 a.m., and the crowds remain rambunctious until 3:00 or 4:00 a.m. (which for some of us can make the standard rooms at the back of the resort a blessing in disguise). *The Sand Bar* adjacent to the to the dining room is supposed to be "quieter" in the evening but it didn't seem noticeably so since every night was cabaret night. Even floor shows and dress up nights were loud and the crowd boisterous.

This is a beautiful island blessed with natural adaptation for water sports and sightseeing. Regrettably the Great Keppel resort is not operated to take advantage of this bounty. First of all, when we asked at reception whether there are day trips by plane or boat to the Outer Barrier Reef, we were told that "the reef is 50 miles away" (actually it's more like thirty miles), so there is no activity involving the main reef. (In fact, in this the staff also was in error, since we found that one independent charterer on the island does offer expensive catamaran service to the Outer Reef for $A800, carrying 15 or 16 passengers on a day trip.) This, therefore, is probably the only Barrier Reef resort in Australia which entirely ignores the Barrier Reef. Local Rockhampton and Yeppoon promotional literature suggests that you could probably charter planes or boats along the coast to pick you up on the island and take you to the reef and back. We feel it is wrong, however, that the visitor is required to be on his or her own devices with no Outer Reef activity easily available through the resort.

There are many local water activities handled through the resort's *Keppel Kuatics* on the beach including without charge large two-passenger water tricycles (on which two of you can pedal merrily across the top of the bay), one and two passenger paddle boards, wind surfing, 13' catamarans, and brief coral viewing and snorkeling trips. There is a charge for paraflying and water skiing on days when these activities are offered. For a small charge, they will also deliver you and pick you up by motorboat so you can enjoy any number if very beautiful long sand beaches on the island. You can also hire one of their motor boats for 2, 4 or 6 hours between 9:00 a.m. and 4:00 p.m..

There is also a very pleasant charter yacht, the Binda, available on some days for half-day snorkel and fishing excursion ($A20 per person) or charter ($A200 for the boat for a full day). This is an independent operation not offered through the resort although departing from Keppel Kuatics, so you must take some money to pay the skipper directly and cannot charge the price to your room. Hidden around the sand spit about a half-mile to the north of the hotel is an independent dive shop which also offers short scuba and snorkel excursions via power boat; they reduce their price if you bring your own gear or the snorkel equipment which the resort will lend you. Scuba divers can refill their tanks here also.

There are also regular boat connections from off the beach just past Keppel Kuatics to the underwater observatory (admission $A5) on the adjacent island. The resort promotes a free daily morning *Booze Krooze* which sails around the island with an optional stop at the observatory, and there is an old ferry which plies back and forth from the beach to the observatory every forty-five minutes or so. This observatory, the largest of its kind in Australia, faces the fringing reef on one side and a sunken Taiwanese junk on the other. It offers a chance to view the mid-size fish feeding at the reef and quite large fish living in the sunken wreck.

Away from the beach, the resort has two inadequately maintained asphalt tennis court and an adjacent brand new one. There are archery sessions, cricket matches, volleyball, ping pong, excellent bush walks around the island, and well organized activities for the younger children. It quickly becomes apparent that one of the most favored activities of resort visitors is drinking at the circular bar at the large *Peanut Pool.*

The resort has a snack bar (the *Keppel Kafe*), limited island shop, hairdressing salon, baby sitting for under three year olds arranged through reception, photographer (the *Keppel Klicker*), laundry facilities, , telex and bank available in the reception office and two or three STD pay phones scattered around the resort (expect lines in the evening).

Keppel's brochures pitch to a party crowd, and it works. The resort enjoys roughly 95% occupancy year round, with a heavy concentration of Melbournean youth (over 60% of the patrons are under 35) and vacationers attracted by the cheap air fares and package deals. For seven years, their motto on their posters and stenciled on the tee shirts invited us to "Get wrecked at Great Keppel." Now Australian Airlines has decided to add a new slogan, which asks the magic question "Can your body take a week on Great Keppel?" The assistant manager assured us that the new ad campaign referred to the abundant athletic activities which the resort offers. The new brochure, however, features pictures of a smiling topless girl whom we are assured in the ad is but nineteen years old (but to avoid charges of chauvinism, there is also a suggestive photo of three girls pulling the trunks from a partially obscured but obviously young male guest). Their ad continues,

> *something in the island air makes people's inhibitions drop faster than Newton's apples. Nothing will prepare you for the Keppel Sexual Olympics. Still, Aussie girls are getting a reputation for stamina events, and this could be your chance to prove it's all true. ...The indoor marathon and the relay are popular events (but only for the fit and the dedicated).*

Actually, whatever went on behind closed doors, there was much less topless sunbathing here than at other resorts   such as Hamilton Island and little suggestion of promiscuity. The kids — and that's in reality what most of them really were, albeit some of them rather older *kids*— wore tee shirts with scatological exaggerations stenciled on them, but in the evening donned some of their nicest clothes for dinner. In contrast to the easy sexual theme of the brochures, there is even a dress code in the *Wreck Bar.*

The biggest adventure for many of the young resort guests seems to be ordering fancy tropical drinks or stacking empty beer cans next to the swimming pool.

The sad part about this operation is that it would have been a better Kings Cross nightclub in Sydney or suburban Brisbane resort — perhaps at Surfers Paradise — without wasting such a beautiful island. Sorry Wreckers, Keppel may be *Kute,,* but in our book you can't hold a *Kandle* to Australian Airlines' other resorts, Dunk or Bedarra Islands. We really couldn't see much reason why Americans should go so far out of their way to visit this island, unless the travel opportunities are somehow irresistible or circumstances restrict you to within fifty miles of Rockhampton.

Great Keppel Island
P.O. Box 108
Rockhampton, Qld. 4700
telephone [79] 391 744

Reservations through Australian Airlines

observatory on Green Island

Green Island
•coral viewing
•national park
•bushwalks
•scuba diving
•snorkeling •swimming

This island was sighted but not visited in 1770 by Captain Cook who named it after the *Endeavor's* astronomer Charles Green. Coconuts were planted on the island a century ago to provide food for ship wrecked sailors. It was first actually served commercially in 1899 by the Butler Family who established a ferry connection. The resort is now owned and operated by the Hayles family who run most of the boats which service the island regularly from Cairns.

Green is a true coral cay, composed entirely of pulverized coral washed up by tide and wave action. A very small sand island, Green is roughly two miles long by one mile wide and rises only about ten feet above sea level. As you approach, it looks every bit the prototype palm-crowned desert island of every adventure story ever filmed. Located 16 miles (or so, depending which government travel brochure you read) from Cairns, it is a popular day-visit resort for Northern Queensland. Perched right on the Great Barrier Reef, Green is an excellent spot for snorkeling and, because the reef shelf drops away offshore, for scuba diving.

Green Island is one of a tiny number of developed islands actually located on the Barrier Reef itself. Heron and Lady Elliot Islands are the only other resort islands undeniably on the reef. Lizard Island claims to be part of the reef and is probably close enough to being a true reef island to qualify, but it is a granite continental island and not a true coral cay. The balance of the islands are situated well inside the Outer Barrier Reef.

Classified as a national park, all plants, wildlife, fish and shells on and around Green are protected. The entire island is covered with a mass of trees and light vegetation growing to within a few yards of the shore line. The beaches are white sand.

Getting there

The island is easily reached by several cruise companies on regular service from the Esplanade in Cairns during the mornings. Large launches carrying up to 250 people ($A11.50 round trip), for example, leave at 9:00 a.m. and return at 3:15 arriving back at Cairns at 4:30. A faster service, *Hayles Green Island Express'* ($A23 round trip), departs Hayles wharf daily at 8:30 and 10:30 for a forty minute trip, returning at 2:30 and 4:30. From Marlin Wharf Cruise Center jetty, the 75' twin-hull Coral Seatel ($A12 round-trip, including lunch, coral viewing, some admissions to island attractions) carrying 160 people daily departs Cairns at 9:00 a.m. and returns at 5:00 p.m.

What to do

The **underwater observatory** established in 1954 is the biggest advertised attraction of Green Island and its probably biggest single disappointment. It is a large 70-ton sunken steel chamber with 22 portholes. In truth, this is just a big steel tube sunk in 15 or 20 feet of sea with clams, coral and sea life *imported* into the area. On the surface, outside the gadget and souvenir shop are plainly identified *replicas* of anchors and other debris from wrecks in the area. Truly honky tonk by most any standard. If you enjoy snorkeling, save $3 and — weather   and tide permitting — follow the clearly marked underwater trail laid out for swimming around the observatory in water about 14' feet deep but hugging the jetty and observatory.

If you liked the observatory, then the next stop should probably be **Marineland Melanesia,** described in promotional literature as *"a unique blend of many major zoological exhibits covering half an acre in doors and out. It houses a world renowned collection of primitive art, along with some magnificent species of salt water   crocodiles from the Papua New Guinea region."* The adjacent **Barrier Reef Theater** is an exhibit which tells the life story of Noel Monkman (one of earliest pioneers on the Great Barrier Reef) and also shows films on Barrier Reef subjects.

Low tide exposes miles of the Barrier Reef for exploration. This chance to explore the reef up close is a good reason for making a special trip to Green Island. The opportunity to walk on the reef will depend, however, on weather and tides. If you are planning a day trip to the island, check and make sure the reef will be exposed and accessible that day. Even if wind or tide prevent your walk on the reef, you can expect a pleasant day on a lovely, if crowded, sandy beach well worth the trip if you are in Cairns and have a day to spend seeing a Great Barrier Reef island. It takes but about twenty minutes to walk around the island. The forest is beautiful and full of bird life. You can swim in waters protected by reefs.

Where to stay

Hayles also operates the *Green Island Reef Resort* on the island offering **very** modest — a la 1930's U.S. motel cabins — small air-conditioned accommodations with dining room for 100 guests. The cost of the transfer to the island and back to Cairns is included in the resort charge. *Lodge units* ($A86 per person, includes dinner, bed and breakfast) have double or twin beds, air conditioning, coffee and tea maker and minibar. Rooms are small and also not particularly well serviced. *Tropical units* ($A96, also with dinner, bed and breakfast) are build of red cedar, with a queen size bedroom and separate lounge area and patio.

For guests and day trippers, the central complex of the island contains bars, a souvenir shop, bank, postal facilities, and take-out food service. Meals are rather limited, usually cold at lunch. There is a glass bottom boat service and other facilities to permit enjoying the reef area. There are day cruises available, snorkel gear at the dive shop, water skiing, but no swimming pool. Tank refills and some diving gear are available at the dive shop.

At least one commercial resort reviewer has advised travellers to skip Green or make it a day trip only. It is criticized for being over-commercialized even by Australian standards. Nonetheless, if you enjoy the prospect of a true tropical island and only have limited time in the Cairns area, Green is well worth the easy day trip.

To combine a short visit to Green with another resort island, consider the Fitzroy Flyer which departs from the Esplanade marina in Cairns early in the morning, spends the morning hours and lunch at Fitzroy and makes a two hour side trip to Green before departing for Cairns at 4:15. There is also the Green, Fitzroy, outer reef trip from the Esplanade if you want to cram a great deal of activity into a single day.

Green Island Reef Resort
Green Island, Qld. 4871
[70] 51 4644; telex AA48332   Reservations direct to the resort

Hamilton Island

Hamilton Island

Hamilton Island

•coral viewing •bushwalks •fishing
•golf •scuba diving •anchorage
•tennis •sailing •snorkeling
•windsurfing •swimming

Controversial Australian entrepreneur, promoter and developer (and one-time cycle mechanic) Keith Williams, who sold his Seaworld on the eastern Gold Coast reportedly for more than $A35 million, has been busy rearranging a sizeable island to his own satisfaction. He did this by acquiring the complete leasehold of Hamilton Island, until ten years or so ago undeveloped and unspoiled. This fairly large resort island, though relatively dwarfed by its huge near neighbors to the north, uninhabited Whitsunday and Hook Islands, is situated adjacent to the south coast of Whitsunday Island and 10 miles south-east of Shute Harbour. Without doubt, this has been the most controversial island resort of the Whitsundays, in fact in Queensland — and perhaps even all Australia, at the moment.

This fairly new resort (the official grand opening was December 1984) is entirely Keith Williams' brain child. Having leased the island originally to establish a deer farm, Williams, after the death of his original business partner, began constructing the resort. For some reason, Australia's usually vocal conservationists remained relatively silent while Williams dynamited the top off the island's tallest peak to make it a helicopter landing site, dredged out a modern boat harbor and marina, filled in the entrance to one of the larger bays, undertook construction of a huge crushed rock seawall because low tide leaves Catseye beach without adequate salt water swimming capability for several hours a day, blew the side off one of Hamilton's hills to extend the runway of his airport so that jets could land [making this the only Great Barrier Reef island currently able to handle jets; in fact Hamilton can handle larger jets up to the new Boeing 767), and started building mid- and high-rise condominiums. Cynics point out that Williams' friendship with Queensland's perpetual premier, Sir Joh Bjelke-Petersen, certainly didn't hurt when it came to quieting any critics of his massive island remodelling job.

Marketing genius that Williams is, he sells his condos before construction commences. The already-completed condos sold at prices ranging from $A140,000 to 250,000, with units in the first 14-story highrise beginning at $A176,000 and increasing $1000 per floor. The latest 17-story building which went up on top of one of Hamilton's hills has one luxury unit per floor and sold with prices starting at $A750,000. Former Beattle George Harrison has acquired five acres of beach on Hamilton for something in the range of $A750,000 and has a private retreat there.

Plans call for several more condominium buildings, an entire small town for staff with schools for their   children and shopping facilities for their families, more than a dozen restaurants including take-out food stands, and a maximum guest population anywhere from three to five thousand people. Williams' own palatial home — with private helicopter pad, enough interior marble to outfit several churches, a basement pistol shooting range — is very prominent on the bluff above the resort. Rumor has it that after several years of construction it has yet to be completed to the owner's satisfaction.

Getting there

Ansett Airlines, owner of nearby Hayman resort, is a major investor in Hamilton Island, which perhaps helps explain why only Ansett and not Australian Airlines (ex- TAA) provides daily direct jet air service with Boeing 737s and 767s from Melbourne (three hours), Sydney (two hours) and Brisbane (one hour twenty minutes). From Brisbane the undiscounted fare is $A245. Service from Cairns — some days by jet (55 minutes), others by F27 turboprops (one hour forty minutes) — is $A147.

Americans flying to Australia via Qantas on excursion or other incentive fare tickets get a thirty percent reduction on Ansett if travelling more than 1000 kilometers or 600 miles on the same carrier; the trips from Sydney to Hamilton, or Brisbane to Cairns with a stop in Hamilton, qualify for the discount. (The same discount applies on Australian Airlines but that carrier doesn't fly to or from Hamilton.) Ansett also flies from Mackay ($A70) and Rockhampton ($A126) daily except Wednesday. Service is also available from Proserpine ($A50), Shute Harbor airstrip ($A40) and Townsville ($A113). There are more than thirty-five direct flights weekly to Hamilton.

Luxury catamarans — the *Hamilton Quick Cat* and *Hamilton Big Cat* — provide rapid connection from Shute Harbor ten miles away by water. Arrival and departure   transit is free for guests staying at the resort. There are also day trips from Shute to Hamilton ($A12.50 each way, departing Shute Harbor at 9:00 a.m. and 5:15 p.m., and from the resort at 7:45 a.m. and 4:30 p.m.) via the Quick Cat II. As a result of Williams' large-scale remodelling, the island boasts an excellent but very expensive anchorage, with a floating marina which ultimately will provide berths for 400 yachts. Hamilton is also the access point for South Molle Island, recently acquired by Ansett, via catamaran or water taxis which meet the flights.

Hamilton Island—"bures"

Where to stay

The *Outrigger Resort*, the first resort (Williams has plans for a second, Mediterranean style resort on a different beach), overlooks Catseye Beach and includes fifty bungalows — prefabricated wood cabins with metal roofs; a bland exterior three-story block of luxury resort suites; mid- and high-rise condominium apartments leased back to the management concern for operation as hotel and resort facilities. The landscaping, including large expanses of carefully maintained lawns and abundant palm trees, does give the resort generally a very attractive appearance, distracting from the rather plain design of most of the residential buildings. Hamilton was among the first Barrier Reef resorts to shift to separate charges for accommodations and meals and has abandoned the full board inclusive fare.

Outrigger's accommodations are a study in contradiction. From the exterior one expects little, yet the interiors are as elegant as the outside is drab. Free-standing Polynesian style *bures* (pronounced "BUR- ay", from the Melanesian name for a hut) and hotel rooms in the four story *Allamanda Lodge* (both $A160 per day per couple, $A30 for a third person) or beachfront suites in the *Bougainvillaea Lodge* ($A190, $A30 for a third or fourth person) and fully self-contained condominium apartments ($A195 per day for 1 bedroom for up to four guests, $A30 for a fifth person; $A275 per day for 2 bedroom for up to five guests, $A30 for a sixth) are luxuriously appointed in contrast to other Barrier Reef resorts. *Allamanda* is getting a bit weary and could use some refurbishing; its large patios don't get sun during winter months, so for now the *bures* are probably the better choice for a couple. The resort has daily standby rates ($A120-180 per couple) for up to three nights on a space available basis for reservations within 48 hours of arrival.

Each *bure* and hotel suite features king size and single bed (two queen beds in the beachfront *Bougainvillaea Lodge),* comfortable conversation area, both ceiling fans and air-conditioning, attractive rattan and wood corner bar with bar sink (except for *Allamanda),* glassware, and fully stocked bar refrigerator, well decorated spacious bathrooms (a few of the earlier *bures* with shower over tub, but most with huge tile showers and double sinks, all with wall-mounted electric hair dryers and an ample supply of fine toiletries), radio, color TV, direct dial ISD and STD phones, and a small veranda or patio. Condominium apartments have one or more bedrooms, full kitchen, washers and dryers, and all of the other appointments of the hotel rooms. There are also guest laundry facilities in each building. A unique feature of Hamilton Island is that there are four specially designed paraplegic rooms, and all ground floor rooms plus tower rooms with elevators are wheelchair accessible. Since paths are paved, this is the only Barrier Reef resort island on which a guest using a wheelchair can enjoy a holiday with minimal difficulty.

In September 1987 construction started on *Hamilton Towers.* It is scheduled to be completed in early 1989 with 400 rooms, ten suites and two penthouses. This self-contained property will have a restaurant, cocktail lounge and convention center.

Hamilton is easily the largest among Great Barrier Reef resorts. Next to luxurious Hayman Island, it also ranks as the most nicely appointed. Interiors are very well decorated — attractive grass cloth walls, excellent tile work, nice interior wood. And nobody seems to care that the exterior architecture is rather bland by contemporary standards or that severe highrise buildings will stick out too obviously and be visible from other islands in the area for miles around, with little hope that landscaping will conceal these fundamentally plain buildings.

What to do

The harbor is situated across the island from the resort and is already one of the finest in North Queensland with berths for over 200 boats. For arriving yachts, mooring prices start at $A30 per overnight, depending upon the length of the boat. Hamilton is also base for *Hamilton Island Charters* offering attractive modern seven- or eight- berth yachts 40' and up (approximately $A400-450 per day plus fuel and provisions) and motor cruisers ($A350-500 per day plus fuel and provisions) for six persons for bareboat charter for overnight or extended rental. Crewed charters ($A700-4000 per day) for four to twelve passengers are also available. Management proudly notes that their charters are more luxurious than those from their across the bay competitors. For *boaties* arriving on their own craft, Hamilton also boasts a fully operational shipyard where you can have your reefer fixed, your hull cleaned or your engines repaired.

Mariner's Inn at the marina includes a restaurant, bar and disco night club upstairs, and downstairs the casual and thoroughly enjoyable *Barefoot Bar*, a jumping tavern serving snacks as well as a full range of refreshment and jammed with resort guests and *boaties*. On the second floor is the *Veranda Room*, another snack style lunch and dinner spot. There is also a general store downstairs selling food supplies, soft drinks, sundries, and the like. Along the road past the harbor there is also a bottle shop with nicely moderate prices, a fish store — also offering fish and chips and similar hot specialties for take-out lunch or dinner, a bakery, H2O Sportz dive shop and resort shops, a pharmacy and even the office of a chartered accountant! Across the road Trader Pete's sells souvenirs, casual clothing

beach on Hamilton Island

and beach gear, magazines, books, hats and post cards. And new construction is still going on around the marina.

There still is an animal farm on the island, and Williams has added a small if uninspiring zoo — a *fauna park* ($A5 per person; free if you buy the $A10 van tour of the resort) — which now has the animals in rather nondescript enclosures. There are a few sleepy koalas in a small structure, and a smattering of emus, peacocks,   wallabies, crocodiles, kangaroos and a wallaroo in a fenced enclosure. The zoo is quite distant from the resort itself, so be prepared for quite a hike if you undertake to walk. The only thing we found particularly to commend the trip — either on foot or by car — were the exceptional views of   the Whitsunday Group from the heights of Hamilton.

The bird life free on the island is terrific: dozens of sulphur crested cockatoos, black crows the size of chickens, flying foxes hanging sleepily from hillside trees during daylight, and an endless supply of hysterical cookaburras.

Back at the resort, you will find the public rooms — the lobby, reception, bar and dining room — to be   particularly attractive. Very high ceilings, split levels, thoughtful attention to decor, and skillful use of tropical woods mixed with sophisticated tiles and fabrics makes for an elegant and very comfortable structure.   Three captive dolphins live in an adjacent pool.   The main resort also includes an arcade of very attractive stores, including some rather elegant up-scale offerings in *Lady Hamilton's* (Cartier jewelry, for example) and *Rosemary's Boutique* (elegant swim and pool wear).

There are several restaurants and food outlets on Hamilton.   Breakfast is available in the *Dolphin Room*, the main dining area. *Continental* ($A10.50) includes a variety of fresh fruits, toast, sweet rolls, juices and coffee or tea; the *complete* breakfast ($A15.50) is for those who want to add the hot table offerings of eggs and meats.   There is also a small adjacent coffee shop with a la carte selections continuously from 10 a.m. until 10 p.m.   Walk around the swimming pool to *Frenchy's Beach Bar & Grill* for an a la carte breakfast from $5.50 for the continental to $9.50 for omelettes and the like.

At the main resort, you can eat à la carte lunch at *Frenchy's* next to the swimming pool, with selections such as sandwiches or salads ranging from $A7.50 to $A12.50.   The coffee shop is also open for sandwiches and snacks.

A short walk over the hill, lunch at the yacht harbor is a challenge to the imagination.   *Wally's Delicatessen* and *The Bakery* both offer sandwiches; the aroma of bread and desserts in the latter makes it hard to escape with just a snack, however.   *Chung Shan Yuen* is open for lunch and dinner and provides an adequate Chinese meal ($A10-21 per main dish).   At the *Fish Market*, aside from buying fresh fish, you can get fish and chips and other fried fresh fish snacks and fresh salads of lobster or giant prawns. There are a few tables in front.   In addition, the resort has thoughtfully scattered picnic tables around the lawns fronting the marina.   The restaurant upstairs at the *Mariner's Inn* has take-out snacks such as fried fish, sausages and hamburgers.   The *Pink Pizza* provides superb pizzas (medium $A7 - 11.50; large $A11 - 14.50) as well as a selection of Italian lunches such as spaghetti, chicken and even osso buco (prices ranging from $A9.50 - $A11.50) and a liter of wine ($A8) or a selection from the wine list ($A16-18).   Most of   the food outlets at the marina also have delivery service to your room ($A3 extra).

Dinner is available all over the island, resort and harborside. The *Dolphin Room*, the resort's central main   dining area, is far more elegant with its very high ceilings and completely open sides.   It offers a varied menu with unusual seafood presentations, porter house or filet steaks, smoked lamb, guinea fowl or chicken, and veal steak at prices from $A17 to $26 for main courses.   The restaurant offers an ambitious if small dessert menu ($A6-11.50), with hazelnut and chocolate mouse, or passion fruit souffle in a pastry shell floating in a pool of marble chocolate, or cream caramel with strawberries and cream.

Frenchy's, next to the pool, has a basic dinner menu with evening specials such as barbecued lamb ($A18.50) or roast duck ($A19.50). A pianist entertains diners in this open-air grill room.

On our earlier visit we had found the *Outrigger Room*, next to the *Allamanda Lodge*, a very satisfactory if slightly uneven seafood restaurant. Because of its newness — it   was one of the first restaurants on Hamilton — we recommended it in spite of its inconsistencies.   The restaurant uses overhead fans for air circulation and is a pleasant tropical wood room with understated decor and good spacing between tables. Service is still eager and friendly.   Regrettably on our latest visit the kitchen had not maintained its standards, while prices had zoomed.

There is a small selection of fresh fish dishes and steak for those not hungry for seafood. The *Outrigger Room's* introductory courses are quite expensive. A small salad with chevre, walnuts, fruits and vegetables was $A14.50. The menu doesn't list a dinner salad, but we were told we could sacrifice the vegetables with our maincourse and substitute a salad if we wished. Dinner for two, with an entrée and main course and a bottle of wine from their unfortunately over-priced list can easily add up to $A100 or more. Be sure to ask the price of such specialties as Moreton Bay bugs or Queensland mud crabs before ordering, for they are considerably more expensive than the other menu selections. Because of unavailability of different fish, the verbal corrections were longer than the printed menu. **Beware:** when the menu describes fish cooked in olive oil and tomatoes, the chef means fish served in a pool of olive oil. Wines from the small list begin at about $A20 and were rather pricey by Australian standards.

In the Marina, the *Mariners Inn Tavern* has a wide variety of grills and seafood. The *Fish Market* serves take out or delivered food until 8:00 pm, and the *Pink Pizza* is open until 11:00 pm.

Our favorite place for dinner was *Ristorante Corsaro*, the harborside Italian restaurant next store to the *Pink Pizza*. A nice antipasto plate or half-order of pasta (about $A8) followed by veal scalloppine or a chicken dish such as cacciatore or valdostana (main courses $A16.50) seemed to us about the best the island offered. You can have pasta as a main course ($A11.50 - 13.50). Australian and Italian wines are offered by the carafe ($A8 - 10) or from the moderately priced list. Try the powerful garlic bread, but only if everyone in your party is in the mood!

Yet to come on Hamilton are another bistro and a Japanese restaurant. Perhaps the highest accolade we can pay to food on Hamilton is to its diversity, both in type and price. This is one of very few resorts where you can control your own food budget and still expect to enjoy yourself.

Unlike most barrier reef resorts, Hamilton boasts a considerable variety in night life offerings. There is a guitarist at *Corsaro*, a pianist at the *Dolphin Room* and *Frenchy's*, a piano bar in the *Captain Cook* bar, Wednesday Polynesian shows and dinner in the *Endeavour Room*, a singer at the *Barefoot Bar*, and plenty of sound at *Durty Nellie's Disco* — where the action goes all night — with a champagne lounge separated from the stage by glass partitions for those who prefer to relax a bit more quietly.

Hamilton Island has outgrown its *bore* water (that is, well water) supply. During our visits the tap water was so loaded with salt-flavored minerals as to be undrinkable. We were told that four major dams and several subsidiary dams (including two for unprocessed water to be used for landscaping and gardening) have been constructed to catch rain water. This increased capacity insures that in most years drinking water need not be imported from the coast. A small plastic pitcher dubbed *rain water* was left in our room each day, but health requirements specifying the addition of chlorine to the rain water meant that it too has a mineral taste. The coffee in the breakfast dining room unfortunately tasted as if it has been made with salty tap water. We hope that improved technology and generous rainy seasons solve this problem and that adequate provision is made for more appetizing drinking water, but we still wonder what will happen in dry years when the island's population hits four or five thousand.

Idleness is not a problem at Hamilton, although it is a temptation. The resort boasts a large fresh water swimming pool with a central island bar. There is a small sheltered jacuzzi on the artificial island in the middle of the pool. Activities include six tennis courts ($A10 per hour; $A2 to rent rackets, balls or shoes) on your choice of asphalt or astroturf and a complete gymnasium facility with squash courts, spa, sauna facilities and exercise classes. At the beach there is a full aquatic sports facility with wind surfing, catamaran sailing, parasailing, snorkeling, water-skiing — all with instruction included in the hire cost — fishing dinghy, outrigger canoe, and *war canoe*. All of these activities, except surf skis and outrigger canoes, do have a fee involved.

Guests on the island can rent Yamaha golf carts for getting around the resort for $A15/hour or $A45/day. There is also a charge for archery as well as for the golf trip to neighboring South Molle Island. (A Hamilton golf course is a possibility in a few years.) You can trek to Passage Peak at the east end of the island or just lie on the beach. You won't have to move a muscle to keep fortified with liquid refreshment; the red *boozemobile* runs along the beach serving the beverage needs of Catseye sun soakers.

There are several off-island activities offered regularly including access to the Outer Barrier Reef. Hamilton Air operates *Jet Ranger* charter helicopters three times a day which serve the barge which the resort has moored at the reef ($A100 per person) allowing two hours for coral viewing, snorkeling, and reef walking. There are also *adventure* ($A45 per person) and *scenic* ($A25 per person) flights of the Whitsundays.

The *Hamilton Catamaran 2001* on Tuesdays and Fridays at 9:45 a.m. takes you for the two hour trip and two hours on the Reef ($A65 per person) for swimming, coral viewing, scuba diving by prior arrangement, reef walking (tides permitting) and a very nice light lunch including cold chicken, a nice cheese spread, and sandwiches with excellent fresh rolls. The boat has a full bar, and drinks may be charged to your room. During the trip out or back, have your picture taken ($A4, no room charge) by social director Davvyd with his well trained white cockatoo Henry perched on your head!

There are trips to Dent Island ($A8), a full day sailing trip ($A40), a twilight cruise ($A5), and a trip to Whitehaven beach on uninhabited Whitsunday Island via high speed catamaran ($A12). Game fishing boats may be chartered ($A700-1500 per day locally, $A100-300 extra for trips to the reef) for four to six guests. Hamilton has extensive scuba diving facilities and services. Certified divers may rent full gear ($A35 per day, $A158 for a week) or individual dive items such as regulators ($A8 per day), tanks ($A8), wet suits ($A7) or snorkel gear ($A6). H2O Sportz offers all day dive and snorkel trips ($A55 plus gear; $A150 for an overnight trip), a helicopter dive trip ($A135 plus gear), a one day resort dive course ($A60) with two hours in the pool and an open water dive at a nearby coral reef, a five day open water certification course ($A325).

There is a professionally supervised *Kids Klub* between 9:00 a.m. and 5:00 p.m. with games, swimming, contests, crafts, and hikes for the three to twelve year olds. Baby sitting is also available.

There are already signs that nearby resorts are becoming increasingly dependent upon Williams' jet airport in preference to the more difficult access through Shute Harbor. Moreover Williams is spending huge sums — figures up to $200 million are bandied around — in developing Hamilton. New condominium projects are on the boards as well as more swimming pools and restaurants. The island population will greatly exceed that of any other Barrier Reef resort island, and its facilities and services — including full-time medical staff equipped even to do cosmetic surgery and an in-place medical evacuation facility — makes it unique in Northern Queensland.

"Not as jazzy but more fun," said one Aussie lady of Hamilton on the ride from Hayman. Given all the changes in the Whitsundays — Hayman going distinctly upscale, Ansett buying South Molle, Four Seasons taking over and refurbishing Lindeman, rumors that Australian Airlines ultimately will restore Brampton — it is difficult to predict the future for this adult amusement park. One thing is certain: Hamilton Island is a very busy resort. It has established a definite niche for itself in the resort market and is assuredly a major factor in the future of the Whitsunday Group and of Great Barrier Reef tourism generally.

Outrigger Resort
Hamilton Island
Private Mail Bag,
Post Office Mackay, Qld. 4740

telephone [79] 469 144; telex 48516

Reservations direct to the resort or through Ansett

on Hamilton Island

Haslewood Island
•*no resort*
•*possible pig hunting*

This good-sized island is due east of massive Whitsunday Island. It has no resort. We mention it here because there is reference in local publications to the presence of domestic pigs having been turned loose years ago to run wild on Haslewood for hunting (including recommendations for times and methods to hunt these animals), and you will come across references to this island in publications mentioning the Whitsundays. Our yacht captain who seemed very knowledgeable about all of the Whitsunday Passage islands had never heard of these pigs, however. Although it somehow acquired a reputation for being a good island to sail to, the currents are difficult and the anchorage not very good.

Hayman Island Resort

Hayman Island Resort

Hayman Island

•coral viewing •national park •bushwalks •fishing •waterskiing •scuba diving •anchorage •tennis •golf •sailing •snorkeling •windsurfing •swimming

One look and you just know this resort is expecting an episode of *Lifestyles of the Rich and Famous* to be filmed here. With remodelling costing $A200,000,000 completed Christmas 1987, Hayman Island had been closed from July of 1985 to April, 1987, for one of the most massive overhauls ever undertaken voluntarily by a resort hotel. In a country where many resort islands don't even give you a key or lock doors, Hayman uses a modern electronic key-card system to open guest room doors, and each room has a safe for which customers can enter personal combinations electronically.

Owned by Australia's privately owned Ansett Airlines through its Ansett Hotels subsidiary, this most northerly resort of the Whitsunday group is located about seventeen miles northeast of Shute Harbor and sixty-five miles north of Mackay. Hayman is at the head of the Whitsunday Passage. A national park, all coral and shells are fully protected.

This is probably the best known of islands in the Whitsunday Group if not of all Barrier Reef resorts. Early this century, Hayman Island was leased for a sawmill operation. After 1935 it was operated as a fishing resort, and in 1948 Ansett acquired the lease intending to use the island only as the northern destination for its flying boats. Later the decision was reached by Reginald Ansett to develop a resort here, and the hotel opened in 1950, originally as the *Royal Hayman Hotel* (allowed to be named *Royal* because the Queen was to attend the grand opening, even though circumstances forced her to cancel).

The island is of moderate size and is fairly arid, with a low horseshoe-shaped range of hills behind the resort. The resort side is typical of bush islands. The very pleasant hiking trails are principally on the north side of the island (the back side from the resort) which, because of the way the island faces, is somewhat more rain forest in nature. One of the tracks is a five mile trek around the island, and the shortest is the half mile trek to *Whitsunday Passage Lookout.* Breathtaking southerly views from hilltop and even from the broad sandy beach in front of the resort overlook Hook Island and the Whitsunday Passage and are among the most spectacular among Great Barrier Reef resorts. Around the island you will find wild life and forested ravines, half-mile wide fringing reefs, kookaburras, cockatoos, sea gulls, and lorikeets. Reputedly the first tropical palm tree on the island was planted by novelist Zane Grey, and there are now hundreds.

Getting there

The usual approach to *Hayman Resort* is daily via the *Sea Goddess,* a huge new high speed catamaran ferry serving champagne and canapés during the voyage from Hamilton Island, connecting with the Ansett jet flights from Sydney via Brisbane ($A35 in conjunction with flights). Also accessible via Hamilton Island helicopter ($A155 per person from Proserpine; $A100 per person from Hamilton), there are also periodic launches from Shute Harbor. There are some moorings available for visiting boats (by arrangement with management) in a newly developed protected marina. Whether you arrive by boat or helicopter, guests are transported by van from the jetty and heliport about a   half mile from pier to hotel reception area.

Where to stay

Hayman is the personal project of renowned CEO Sir Peter Abels who, it is said, personally tests design of chairs by using them in his office before approving them. International media magnate Rupert Murdock, half owner of Ansett, has also taken a personal interest in this project, visiting the resort regularly. Scattered profusely throughout *Hayman Resort* are expensive objets d'art such as huge 300 year old Aegean oil jars, Chinese porcelain urns, oriental carpets, Burmese monastery doors. There is an aviary and   tropical garden on the roof of the central building; off   to the side is a pond with black and white swans.

We learned during our guided tour with Michael Reed, group co-ordinator, that the elegant fireplace (fireplace? in the tropics?) in the hallway from the salon to the opulent crystal dining room is a one and a half ton twelfth century French antique, with a Napoleon era fireplate and antique French clock on the mantle. The center piece of the billiard room is the 100 year old table from Melbourne.

Marble, principally Australian, is everywhere — in guest rooms, lobbies, restaurants, and walkways. One of the resort executives confessed he has already slipped and fallen on wet marble and that the resort will have to find some sort of fix for the problem, since the open-air passageways in this water-oriented resort will invariably be wet in places. The public rest rooms in the central reception area would shame the elegant facilities in New York's luxurious *Four Seasons Restaurant;* there is chocolate marble in men's room, while the ladies' room has silk panels on the walls and pink marble floors.

There are three separate reception areas: one in each wing, and the elegant marble central reception for *Beachfront, Garden* and *Palm* rooms. The main entrance road for vans or limousines runs between large reflection ponds. The gorgeous Italian carpet in the reception area cost in excess of half a million dollars.

The elegant guest rooms are outfitted with elegant wood and wicker furniture, some with area rugs like Belgian tapestries, aqua bedspreads

Hayman Island Resort—reception lobby

and cushions, refrigerators, radios (with separate volume control for the bathroom speaker), and television with video cassette player ($A6 charge to rent movies at the desk). There is both air conditioning along with an overhead fan, but we couldn't find the control for the fan. Bathrooms have a hair dryer and double sinks. One discordant note for such luxury: complementary toiletries consisted of rather inelegant shampoo and bath gel; no hair conditioner or moisturizers like those found in other less pricey resorts. Amply equipped for the executive traveller, there were four telephones per room and additional outlets for more. No in-room irons or coffee makers for this top scale resort, however; call housekeeping if the mood to iron or cook overtakes you.

The resort, consisting of blocks of one story and low-rise units, now has 230 guest rooms with at least six distinct types of accommodations, all priced for room only with no meals included: *Garden Court* twins or doubles ($A220 per night) and *Palm Garden* twins or doubles ($A245) are in the old central building over main reception area. These are what pass for base rate rooms in this luxury resort. The new three story *West Wing* (twins and doubles $A250) and four floor *East Wing* (slightly larger twins and doubles slightly higher) flank the central core. There are *West Wing Suites* and *East Wing* one-, two-, and three- bedroom *penthouses* (starting at $A450). The West Wing faces the huge artificial lagoon, while the East Wing fronts ornamental ponds and bridges. Lastly, *Beachfront* twins and doubles ($A290) scattered about the grounds immediately adjacent to the beach are shower-only older units which have been completely redone.

Hayman Resort has five restaurants. The centerpiece is *La Fontaine*, a formal French dining room with Waterford crystal chandeliers and formal service, where manager Christian expects gentlemen to wear jackets and neckties! To the side a private dining room with an elegant rosewood table is available for private parties. With a bottle of expensive Australian wine ($A22 and up) or very expensive French wine expect dinner for two to cost $A100 or more.

In addition to *La Fontaine*, there are the *Planters Restaurant* (Trader Vic's style) seating about 100 people; a *Japanese teahouse* with its bridge over the adjacent carp pond; the casual *Tratorria* open 24 hours a day; and, the very attractive *coffee shop* featuring the resort-made desserts and chocolates. In addition there is light meal service available poolside until 6:00 pm, as well as the room service menu at the lanai adjacent to the West Wing reception area or in your room 24 hours a day. The resort's large wine cellar hosts weekly tastings.

The huge main kitchen houses the hotel bakery, the chocolate factory which turns out beautiful truffles, an ice cream plant, and the resort's own butchery, and the central dining facility's sixty chefs. In addition to this gigantic facility, each restaurant has its own subsidiary kitchen. The island has built its own desalinization plant which processes better than 150,000 gallons of water per day. The process is so thorough that the resort has to depurify the product by adding chemicals.

The entertainment center across the walkway from the restaurant and main reception building has a long granite top bar. Nightly cabaret style floor shows, with such features as a calypso or south seas band, change monthly. Few things remain from the old Royal *Hayman Resort* of before except a very noisy all-night disco thoughtfully situated down the beach somewhat away from most of the guest rooms; *Hernando's Hideaway* — which goes until 4:00 a.m. — is the only place on the resort where staff and guests mix.

Ordinarily the staff of this ultra-modern facility is nearly invisible. The hotel has dug a network of   underground tunnels for the use of staff for such things as food and laundry delivery. If you wonder how a remote resort like this manages to keep friendly and efficient staff with little time off-island, all employees are contracted for twelve months. They receive free room and economical meals, and their inbound airfare is refunded after six months.]

What to do

The bay in front of the *Hayman Island Resort* is virtually completely enclosed by coral reef making the lagoon ideal for swimming, skindiving, snorkeling, water skiing, sailing, paraflying and aqua planing. It is a big bay, but it is definitely full of activity in the afternoons. When the tide is low, however, the bay virtually disappears and the muddy bottom is exposed for a good quarter-mile from the beach. On some days, due to tidal restrictions the beach closes at 1:30 pm!

The bay, nearby small islands and sandy bar offer excellent shallow water snorkeling and scuba diving to sixty feet. The bay has a shallow sloping coral reef, eventually leading out to a vertical wall at forty feet depth, accessible from shore or from Hayman's dive boat. *Dolphin Point*, approached from the dive boat, offers scuba diving from 20-60 feet on rugged terrain from a coral rubble bottom. The resort has full time scuba

Hayman Island Resort

instructors with a complete dive shop and offers a *resort course* permitting next-day diving from their boat or, on some   days, even from the Outer Reef accompanied by an instructor. There are barges moored at the Outer Reef for day visitors and the hotel regularly runs a large boat excursion to the reef for snorkeling and diving. In addition, they have acquired an "Aquascope", a semi-submersible catamaran with a glass bubble hull. This submarine, built in France, is so maneuverable that it can get to tiny parts of the reef without damaging the coral. It carries eight passengers and allows people who don't dive to appreciate the Outer Reef.

Hayman Resort has one indoor and three outdoor tennis courts ($A10 hire fee; rackets $A5 each). The indoor court can be converted to an ice rink overnight; with 280 seats   it can support tennis tournaments as well as ice shows. There is a squash court, a bocce court, and a small spa and sauna with co-ed exercise facilities. Outside the *West Wing* of the hotel is what the resort claims is the largest swimming pool in the southern hemisphere, a salt water lagoon with a fresh water pool in the middle. (Hamilton Island disputes the claim, as does the new Sheraton in Port Douglas with its five acre pool.)

The hotel offers — for separate fees — all water   sports except jet skis. Ansett has acquired a 20% interest in all concessions to insure quality. You will find wind   surfing, snorkeling, hobi-cat, paddle skis, waterskiing, small motor boats, glass bottom boat ride, and paraflying ($A25). There are boat trips to adjacent islands and (as always, weather and tides permitting) to the Outer Reef, and fishing excursions to bring back such catch as coral trout, red emperor, and big game fish like blue fin tuna and black marlin. In the central structure are the new upscale boutiques, a pharmacy, hairdresser, beautician, child care center, art gallery and a photo lab.

It is hard to tell how successful the new *Hayman Resort* will be with visiting Americans. Surely there are luxury resorts much closer to home, and such opulence seems to us more than a little out of place in an otherwise casual, relaxed part of Australia where few people travel with neckties. If, on the other hand, you particularly like a busy vacation at a very elegant resort similar to those you might expect to find in the more upscale Hawaii, Caribbean or European vacation spots, this could be the best place for you to enjoy the Whitsunday Group and the Great Barrier Reef.

Hayman Island
via Proserpine, Qld. 4801

[79] 469 100; telex 48163; telefax [79] 469 100, ext. 786
Reservations through Ansett Airlines

Heron Island—breeding ground for the giant sea turtles

Heron Island
•coral viewing
•national park •bushwalks
•fishing •scuba diving
•anchorage •tennis
•snorkeling •swimming

This breathtakingly beautiful tiny low island — the highest point of land is just about ten feet above sea level— is a particularly strongly protected national park only about one mile in circumference. Heron is a *true coral cay,* an evergreen island made of coral debris and sand, sitting right on the Great Barrier Reef. The only other resorts actually part of the Outer Reef are Green and Lady Elliot Islands. Green is primarily for day trips, and Lady Elliot on the Reef is more a camping facility than a true island resort. Lizard, a continental island, is geographically very close to the Outer Reef but not an integral architectural part of it. Covered by a Pisonia forest grown to a height of almost 50 feet and by groves of Pandanus and Casuarina near the beaches, with coconut palms, oaks, coral, sand and grass, both from a distance and up close Heron Island looks just like the proverbial tropical desert island.

Heron Island is situated in the Capricorn Group, 43   miles northeast of Gladstone. It was first charted in 1843 and was named because of the presence of distinctive white, black and gray herons. Although the home of untold thousands of birds, the island is perhaps best known as a breeding ground of giant sea turtles. One of the island's first commercial enterprises, in fact, was the establishment in 1925 of a turtle soup factory and cannery which also marketed   tortoise shell products with little regard for depletion of these venerable and rather scarce animals. In 1932 an attempt was made to establish a resort on the island, but after World War II the effort foundered somewhat. The island had become a marine national park in the 1940's, and in 1974 P & O Australia bought an interest in the resort and assumed full control of the resort lease in 1979, upgraded and refurbished most of the facilities and established the water desalinization system for the resort.

The waters surrounding Heron Island are a paradise for divers (both scuba and snorkel) and for photographers. Manta rays, angelfish, cod — 1150 species of sea life in all swim in these waters.   Surrounded by approximately 10 square miles of what well *may be the best, most easily accessible coral beds of the entire Barrier Reef region,*   Heron undoubtedly offers visitors the best reef experience of all Barrier Reef resorts within the least distance from your hotel room.   At low tide visitors walk on part of the 15 miles of surrounding Great Barrier Reef without taking a plane or hour-long boat ride as with other resorts.

Getting there

Getting to Heron is itself something of an adventure. Air Queensland has several daily flights to Gladstone connecting with Australian Airlines and Ansett services in Brisbane ($A119 each way), Townsville ($A179), Bundaberg ($A32), Mackay ($A120), Proserpine ($A141) or Rockhampton ($A55).   From Gladstone, the most practical method of reaching Heron Island is via the Helitrans Bell Jet-Ranger   4 passenger or Alouette 6 passenger helicopter from Gladstone airport ($A140 per person each way), an exciting thirty to forty minutes, during which the airline provides you with stereo earphones which eliminate most of the engine noise, through which they play a classical music background accompanied by a commentary from your pilot [they used to have a beautiful recording prepared by the late Richard Burton, but evidently no longer use it] describing the exceptional marine scenery along the way.   Flights operate between 9:00 a.m. and 3:00 p.m., connecting with scheduled commercial traffic to Gladstone, according to load and not fixed schedule.   There is a fairly strict one suitcase limit if the copters are running full.

If you prefer the less expensive approach or just must carry more gear than the helicopter will handle,   there is now an air-conditioned launch service operated by P & O from O'Connell Wharf in Gladstone, departing 8:00 a.m daily except Thursday ($A50 each way, 2 1/4 hours), but be aware that this crossing can be VERY choppy.   Regrettably   for *boaties*, Heron has a poor and very restricted anchorage for yachts, and it's unfortunately a long row ashore, so there isn't much business from charter or private yachts.

Where to stay

Don't count on getting stand-by reservations at *Heron.* It is more often than not fully booked. It has only ninety rooms, accommodating up to 280 guests in motel-type lodges with modern built-ins and reasonably comfortable appointments. Three types of hotel accommodations are available: *lodges* ($A89 per person per day, all meals included) have share facilities and *Reef Suites* ($A135) have private baths. *Heron Suites* ($A158) also have private facilities, a balcony overlooking the beach in upstairs units, quarry tiled floors with rugs, higher ceilings and more comfortable cross-ventilation for hot or muggy days. All units have overhead fans, refrigerators, and the ubiquitous tea and coffee making facility. Some rooms have patios. One or two persons may stay in an exclusive *beach house* which the resort offers ($A325). No camping facilities exist on the island, and because of the distance to the coast there is no mechanism for day visits.

What to do

One of the first unique things which you will encounter on this naturalists' living museum island is the gooney but entirely fascinating migratory *mutton bird* which regularly returns to the island from Siberia in late October and leaves exactly five months later. These duck-sized creatures — called mutton birds because the flavor of their fatty meat reminded early sailors of the familiar (to them) taste of mature sheep — are a constant source of amusement on the island. They have so much trouble taking off, staggering down the beach almost in a drunken lurch until they gain enough speed to fly that they are very amusing to watch. They are excellent flyers and will stay out all day fishing the reef. When they return in the night hours and try to land, however, more often than not they will bump into something to stop their flight: trees, the ground, or surprised resort guests. They live in nests burrowed under the roots of the tropical trees and make a meowing noise all night that sounds like a small menagerie of Siamese cats audible as you pass their homes under trees everywhere near the island's beaches.

The pisonia trees are jammed with *noddy terns,* named because their bobbing heads appear to be mounted on springs. These constantly agreeable birds bring these tropical trees to life and also make headgear recommended attire when trekking through the woods during the nesting season. Even if you have never paid much attention to the bird kingdom, it is guaranteed that on Heron Island you will be continually fascinated with the reef herons (after which the island is named), silver gulls, fairy terns, black naped terns, doves, landrails, and incredible variety of other bird life.

The spectacle of the *giant turtles* nesting from late October until March — green turtles, along with a few loggerheads and hawksbills — is one of the most remarkable nature experiences you will ever observe. These giant female turtles drag themselves well up onto the beach, then through some mysterious instinct decide on the best place to lay their eggs, laboriously dig a trench in the sand, lay the several dozen eggs the size of golf balls, cover them with sand, and then ponderously drag themselves back into the sea and swim away, not to return for perhaps fifty years. They are so intent on what they are about that people can stand quietly and watch this amazing spectacle; once the eggs have been laid, the turtles are so docile and unafraid that flashbulbs and the close approach of people don't faze them.

Between six and ten weeks after the eggs have been so painstakingly covered, the tiny hatchlings struggle out of the eggs and undertake to defy the almost impossible odds against reaching the sea, contending first with obstacles and birds ashore, crabs at the shoreline, and then hungry denizens of the sea. Few evidently survive, but those that do will return decades later to repeat this breeding cycle. The turtles have been studied and banded for only a couple of decades; where they go, why they return to this very place, and even exactly how old they are when they produce offspring is still not clearly known.

This is literally an island that's a university. The resort lease covers only one-quarter of the island, with the balance reserved to educational purposes under the auspices of Queensland University. They maintain a substantial facility on the island (a short walk from the resort) and their *Marine Biological Station* displays live specimens of tropical fish and marine life indigenous to the island and its surrounding waters. The staff of the Station is happy to discuss their research with visitors, and a visit to their facility is a must while on the island.

Heron Island hosts a *Skin Divers' Rally* in June and July and *Festival* each November. Quite understandably, this island is a real favorite with scuba divers; the dive shop rents air tanks ($A2 per dive) and some diving gear including regulators ($A4 per dive), buoyancy compensators ($A4), and wetsuits ($A8). Refills ($A4) are available. Although most Australian tour advisers recommend bringing most of your gear, Heron Island warns you if you intend to take the helicopter that carrying space is limited, and your tanks may come on a later flight when space is available — perhaps days later and suggests planning to rent tanks on the island.   The resort operates two daily snorkel and one-tank guided diving trips to Heron Reef, Wistari Reef, Gorgonian or Rubble Banks, departing 9:15 a.m. and 2:15 p.m. for 2 hours ($A10 per scuba diver, $A6 per snorkeler). There are 7- and 10-day dive packages (ranging from $A230-300 in addition to the room rates).   There is a formal seven day scuba diving instruction program ($A200) commencing on Sundays. This must be booked before arrival, however, and requires a medical certificate and two passport sized photos for enrollment.

There is excellent diving as close to the resort as only 250 yards from the boat basin around the *Big Bommie.* The coral bommies 20'to 50' below surface are home to barracuda, kingfish, cod, large trout, variety of tropical fish, delicate fire coral and other beautiful soft corals.   Occasionally outside the fringing reef, one can see humpback whales and killer whales in surrounding waters.

This is an excellent opportunity for some of the world's best underwater photography, particularly since many of the fish have become so tame because they have gotten used to hand feeding. Even the shallow waters off the hotel beaches have thousands of beautiful smaller tropical fishes of all different types. Just walking around the small island and peering into the shallow waters off the backside of the island, you will most likely see the beautiful if somewhat shy rays sporting in the water. Even without the natural life, the soft white sand beaches are an attraction by themselves.

The daily glass bottom boat ($A5 per person) carrying up to 25 passengers takes bags of left-over bread and rolls from breakfast and thereby guarantees that you will   see hundreds of tropical fish, including some giant specimens — with sharp teeth — so do let go of the roll when the big ones jump out of the water for it, and do not try to hand feed them. In fact, the marine life here in general is particularly accessible to human visitors because it has become very spoiled. Outside the reef, for example, there lives a shark which has become too accustomed to the 11:00 o'clock visit from the *garbo man* who takes a skiff out with the daily refuse from the resort kitchen. We were   told that the garbage was late one day, so the shark upended the boat, dumping the startled driver into the water.

But the shark wasn't stupid, just hungry, so he let the chagrinned garbo man off with just this warning not to be late in the future.

The resort also offers a 7 1/2 hour reef cruise for up to 30 passengers ($A18 per person) which gives an excellent opportunity for walking on the reef if the tides are low   enough to inspect the incredible array of animals that live among the coral. This activity is particularly tide and weather sensitive, however, so if reef walking is a principle reason for your visit, be sure to check local tide tables or telephone the resort for tide information to see if the tides will coincide with the dates of your visit.

The staff conducts an outstanding two hour walking tour of the island each morning pointing out and explaining the incredible array of natural life all over the island. Do take this easy walk, but remember to wear a hat! Each year two weeks are set aside specially for the serious naturalist. *Bird Week* (in December of each year) and *Reef Week* (in February of each year).   These involve lectures, discussions, projects and field excursions which are led   by a team of expert lecturers in the fields of ornithology, marine biology and photography; advance registration is essential to participate in these events.

Heron is a reasonably complete resort with other things to do beside enjoying the surroundings — if you have time or energy for other activities after spending hours in the almost hypnotically beautiful waters. There are tennis courts which are more often than not in terrible shape so not for the serious player; a friend of ours calls this "hit and giggle" tennis. A couple of times a week there are day cruises to nearby islands for a day on   the beach, snorkeling from the beach of a different island, and a popular barbecue luncheon. Fishing trips to waters outside the limits of Heron Island National Park are available   aboard the 35' M.V. Christine ($A15 per person for half day, $A25 full day, gear included) where you may catch groper, kingfish, mackerel, red emperor, coral trout, coral cod and sweetlip.

The resort does not have the usual collection of   catamarans, windsurfers, water tricycles, and small motorboats that you might find at other resorts. How ever, there is the swimming pool, volley ball, ping pong, and the usual selection of island resort entertainments.

Dining was not the strongest reason for visiting Heron Island. As with a couple of the other resorts, we were possibly tougher on Heron because — owned as they are by an elegant passenger steamship line — we were given to expect cuisine of particular distinction. Food is definitely abundant and hearty, although perhaps just a bit too contrived. There is a choice of three main courses each evening, but why the chef feels the urge to try to prepare veal Cordon Bleu for two hundred people simultaneously, we cannot fathom. The barbecue steaks and chops are so superior. Unfortunately, again for reasons not clear to us, the fresh fish seemed bland and not as enjoyable as from several other Barrier Reef resort kitchens. We should hasten to point out that dinner is a very social time in the dining commons, and most people sit at larger tables and become acquainted with their fellow visitors. If you can enjoy a hearty and pleasant evening meal, this is indeed a fun time to share the day's superb adventures.

Evening activities in the resort center around the well stocked *Turtle Bar* or the *Pandanus Lounge* disco. There are movies most nights, and there is a live band for dancing two nights a week. The resort is large enough that you will have little difficulty making new acquaintances and sharing experiences over a relaxing drink. The real night life, however, is the natural life, nighttime strolls along the beach — particularly during the summer (December - February) to see the mutton birds and the turtles, to count the myriad stars, to listen to the surf.

Perhaps you have guessed that we very much like Heron Island. To many people, Heron Island is one of the world's truly special places. It is not that the resort is especially luxurious but rather the island itself which just possibly brings the spectacle of nature to you with less effort and in more comfort than anywhere else in the entire world.

Heron Island
via Gladstone, Qld. 4680
telephone [79] 781 488

Reservations through P & O Resorts, 14252 Culver Drive, Suite A-316, Irvine, California 92714;
telephone [714] 786-0119 or [800] 472-5015

rainforest on Hinchinbrook Island

deserted beach on Hinchinbrook Island

Hinchinbrook Island
•coral viewing
•national park •bushwalks
•fishing •waterskiing
•anchorage
•snorkeling •swimming

This tremendous island is the world's largest island national park, more than ten times the size of Manhattan Island and one of the largest islands in the southern hemisphere. Alan Lucas, author of *Cruising the Coral Coast,* described Zoe Bay at the southeast end of Hinchinbrook as

> *perhaps the most beautiful place on the entire east coast of Australia. The beach is gently sloping, hard sand backed by low native scrub interspersed with tropical foliage and palms. In the background, soaring skywards, are the spectacular mountains of Hinchinbrook's backbone.*

From the north end of the island where the resort is situated   there are stunning views of Goold and Brook Islands.

With Dunk Island, *Hinchinbrook* shares the distinction of being one of Australia's two coastal tropical island resorts. The other resorts to the south, until you reach Heron, are all situated on bush islands. Located approximately one hundred miles south of Cairns and an equal distance north of Townsville, it is about fifteen miles off the coast from Cardwell. Because of its massive size, Hinchinbrook from a distance appears to be part of the mainland. It is separated from the mainland, however, by the Hinchinbrook Channel, a long underwater fault valley.

The western edge of Hinchinbrook is characterized by tropical green vegetation with mountains behind. On the eastern side you are overwhelmed with the beauty of palm fringed bays with wide sandy beaches set between rocky headlands. The island is covered with tropical vegetation. It has dense rain forests — one of which is the densest in Australia, six picturesque mountains over 3000 feet tall, abundant wildlife and plunging waterfalls, and mangrove waterways — including one with a plank bridge where scientists from the Australian Institute of Marine

Science (AIMS) are studying the ecology of such groves. All twenty- eight varieties of Australian mangrove have been identified in the Hinchinbrook delta. The mangrove tree is special because, although it grows at the edge of bodies of salt water, it is a fresh water tree. The secret is in its   complex root and leaf system which is a natural desalinization plant — one which man has only recently finally been able to copy in a rudimentary fashion after years of study and experimentation.

Hinchinbrook Island is also the highest on the Queensland coast — 3650 feet at *Mount Bowen,* and the western half is where Australia's highest rainfall is recorded. The island has no permanent inhabitants other than the resort operators. Remnants of stone fish-traps and cave paintings indicate that Aboriginals lived there   at least seasonally. The decision has been made by Australian authorities and the resort operators to preserve this national natural treasure, so very little additional development will take place even in conjunction with the resort property.

Hinchinbrook is somewhat difficult to reach.   The resort has no airfield and no intention of building one. From Cairns there is 7- or 13-passenger sea plane service ($A104) landing near the resort jetty on Wednesdays and Saturdays aboard Reef World Airline (formerly Air Whitsunday). From Townsville Reef World flies ($A92) on Monday, Wednesday, Friday, Saturday and Sunday. Interestingly, Hinchinbrook is thus coincidentally one of the very few barrier reef resorts with a direct air connection to another resort island, solely because the seaplane service out of Townsville makes an intermediate stop at Orpheus Island on the way to Hinchinbrook — and after Hinchinbrook from Cairns — if there is a reserved passenger, although neither resort advertises this link. Reef World service also connects with that from the Whitsunday Group, so you can string together flights to Hinchinbrook from Airlie Beach or Hamilton Island ($A193).

Getting there

If you are not approaching Hinchinbrook by air from   Cairns or Townsville (or Orpheus) the problem is getting to Cardwell conveniently. The town lies roughly midway   between Townsville and Cairns; driving time is approximately two and a half hours on the good quality two-lane Bruce Highway. Once there, opposite the island and roughly fifteen miles away, launches to the island ($A26 per person round   trip) depart from the jetty at 9:00 a.m. for the short ride to the resort daily except Monday. (Monday is the *quiet* day on this quietest of islands, with no scheduled arrivals or departures or formal activity.) The return from the resort is daily at 4:00 p.m. If you must get to or depart from the resort at some other hour you can charter the resort boat ($A200) or talk to Bonnie at the Hinchinbrook booking agency next to the post office in Cardwell about chartering one of the many other boats ($A136) which work Hinchinbrook channel for a one way pick-up or delivery at the resort.

There are also boat cruises operating from Cardwell to the northern (resort) section of the island and coastal cruise service from Cardwell to Lucinda through the spectacular channel. You can also hire a bareboat or houseboat at Cardwell; the usually calm waters of the Hinchinbrook Channel provide safe boating even for inexperienced sailors, and the charter operators provide necessary basic training prior to departure.

For people sailing to Hinchinbrook, Zoe Bay — although incredibly beautiful — makes a rather poor anchorage because of its exposure to the rather steady south-easterlies. Ramsey Bay on the eastern side can be approached directly by sail along the east coast of the island, providing a safe sheltered anchorage, or by motor from the resort through the western mangrove estuaries and then by foot across a short boardwalk the rest of the way through the mangroves, then on a path through ti tree forests to the sand dunes of Ramsey Beach. On this beautiful six-mile long beach you will often find petrified crabs and lovely shells.

If you have any difficulty planning your transportation to or from Hinchinbrook, however, fear not, for the resort staff is incredibly understanding and helpful in seeing to it that guests arrive and depart as conveniently and inexpensively as possible. Should you be sailing (motor or sail), Hinchinbrook invites *boaties* and offers excellent anchorage as well as fuel (if you order ahead).

Where to stay

The resort at Cape Richards is set above Orchid Bay, a beautiful bay beach by anyone's standards, situated on the northernmost tip of the island. When you step from your boat, plane or launch, you will be warmly greeted by the island's most genial and helpful young managers, Geoff and Marie Gray. Under new management in 1987 the staff has stabilized and boasts kitchen and house staff with longer stays than most other barrier reef resorts. This incredibly rustic resort has a knack for attracting exceptionally pleasant and friendly employees.

While Geoff and Marie invite you into the restaurant/bar/commons next to the fresh water swimming pool for a cool refreshment on arrival, the company truck will transport your luggage to one of fifteen bungalows — eleven large self-contained forest units ($A150 per person per day, with all meals; children 4 to 14, $A50), some with filtered sea views through the trees, with double and two single beds in one room, bath room in the center, and lounge and living room area with a large refrigerator, a kitchen sink, counter, table and day bed in the other   room. There are four divided "half-cabin" bungalows ($A120 per person per day, all meals). (Reef World Airlines — formerly Air Whitsunday — offers a *super saver island stand-by holiday* at Hinchinbrook, departing from Cairns on Wednesdays with three nights for $A395 and on Saturdays for four nights for $472, air fare included.) The rooms are very simple and very rustic — ceiling fans but no air conditioning, no television, no newspapers, no radios, no telephone, no distractions.

What to do

After meeting your hosts and the resort staff and inspecting your accommodations, you will be offered the chance to have another drink, try the beaches, take a walk through the forest, use their water sport facilities or just be lazy. Whatever you decide, the staff will display an uncommon and continuing friendly interest in your enjoying yourselves to the maximum.

Having undoubtedly taken a prompt liking to this friendly place, you will be pleased to discover that the meals are quite an unusual dining experience. The very creative chef has real talent. Serving a wide variety of popular dishes in the nouvelle or California cuisine style, he also produces a weekly barbecue—our personal favorite—on the terrace next to the pool with such delicacies as marinated shrimp grilled on the barbie, mackerel or other channel fish with a coconut cream sauce, marinated steaks grilled to your taste, and a delicious variety of fresh salads. For such a tiny facility the resort also boasts a   fine Australian wine list and well stocked bar.

Morning and noon meals are served in or outside the dining room, although they will gladly prepare a small   continental breakfast for the following morning which you may take back to your room after dinner.

They offer a picnic lunch (somewhat skimpy and rather unimaginative and the only thing we would hope they might improve upon), for when the mood strikes you to explore other parts of this huge national park or picnic on one of the beautiful empty beaches. Like everything   else here, dress at mealtime is super casual.

Around the dining area, you will almost certainly have 'Bee or another of the friendly wallabies (often with a *joey,* or baby, which continues to live in her pouch until perhaps six months of age) politely inquiring if you have any extra scraps of bread or melon rind for a snack. The older wallabies, particularly the males, become quite territorial and ordinarily leave the commons area. The younger ones, however, delight in visiting the tourists.   It was recently discovered that bread or anything with flour is very dangerous and possibly even fatal to the wallabies. We are assured it

a wallaby on Hinchinbrook Island

is perfectly all right to continue to feed 'Bee or his friends scraps of vegetables or *paw paw,* but resist the temptation to give them your morning toast. Save that for Sly, the enormous groper fish at the end of the jetty who gobbles the garbage at 7:00 a.m. every morning.

In addition to these small marsupials, you will see a few *goanas* —what we call iguanas—also known as   monitor lizards, perhaps two or three feet in length. They are quite shy and will give you a wide berth. Locals will advise you that when alarmed the monitor lizard makes for the nearest tree on the run and will climb out of danger. if you encounter one out in the bush where, unlike Hinchinbrook, there are no nearby trees, old timers tell you that you must flap your arms and wave your hands so these poor lizards won't mistake you for a tree and try to climb you with their rather sharp claws. A variation on this story advises you to "hit the ground real quick "if the goana runs at you so he won't think you're a tree.

The beach just down the hill from the restaurant area is one of the most beautiful in Great Barrier Reef country and indeed one has to look carefully even in the United States to find such beaches, particularly with such a tiny (and often entirely invisible) occupancy. The sand runs well into the ocean, unlike the mud flats that are exposed around other Barrier Reef islands at low tide, and there is reasonably good snorkeling around the rocks at the end of the beach.

Remember, though, that this is a national park and natural life is left entirely alone, including the sand flies and other insects. It is well worth the small investment to stop in the shop behind the bar and pick up a bottle of Rid or some other effective insect repellant   cream as soon as you check in, and use it promptly and generously during your stay on Hinchinbrook.

There are laundry facilities available.   Phone calls must be made or received on the island phone in the office. There is a small souvenir and sundries shop next to the office. There is no disco, no band, no movies, no TV, no   room radios, no intrusion into your enjoyment of the national park.

The resort has no social director and no organized activities and doesn't need any.   There are occasional day trips available depending upon tide and weather conditions Occasionally the resort conducts an excursion by boat to *Freshwater* ($A27) where the mountain streams run into the salt water mangrove swamps.   On another day there may be a boat ride through mangrove creeks over to *Ramsey Bay* ($A27) or a half-day trip to the *boardwalk* ($A16) where research continues on the mangroves.   A *reef fishing trip* ($A70) depends on weather, as does the full day cruise to beautiful *Zoe Bay* ($A37).

This is one of the world's great relaxation and nature paradises.   The resort provides paddle surfboards, windsurf equipment, and a canoe. You can fish from the rocks or their pontoon.   There are dinghies for hire ($A30) which allow you to go from the jetty around to explore the mangrove swamps on your own.   They will take you by boat ($A27) over to the nearby *Brook Islands* for outstanding snorkeling within the protected fringing reef and lazing on an outstanding beach.   For sheer abundance of fish and variety of underwater life, the small ecosystem around Brook rivaled that seen anywhere in northeast Australia!   The water is relatively shallow (less than ten feet in the fringe reef area) and quite calm.   This is excellent snorkeling country by any standard.

The staff will direct you to the best paths for bush walking where you can sit in the forest and observe some of the three hundred different species of birds that inhabit the island.   If you are lucky you will see the blue *Ulysses butterflies* or the *Cairns wanderer* and at Turtle Bay some *giant turtles*. About forty-five minutes from Macushla Point — a somewhat rough walk requiring a guide through mangrove swamp and rain forrest — you will see a large example of a *strangler fig tree*. This one tree which must be two hundred years old has branches which seem to span acres. Twined among the huge branches are hundreds of crows nest orchids. Among the mangroves are "ribbon" and brown orchids.

Camping is allowed on the island at Macushla Point on the west side of the island, at Ramsey Beach and Zoe Bay on the eastern side. (A permit is required and may be obtained at the National Parks office just next to the jetty in Cardwell.) There are toilets at Macushla Bay; the other sites lack facilities, and none has any fresh water supplied, although during the summer rainy season fresh water is usually abundant.

For years *Hinchinbrook Resort's* motto is that the maximum population of the island is thirty people (although they may be forgiven for not including children of guests in this census, thereby allowing a massive population explosion to fifty or so when the island is fully booked). We understand, however, that a people boom may be in the works — to sixty guests by replacing some of the bungalows and refurbishing others. Rumor has it that a new dining commons and lounge area quite possibly may be built on the present site of an observation platform overlooking Orchid Beach, with beautiful new timber and rattan cabins behind. The relative impact on this 231 square mile island would be perhaps one additional person per twenty-five wallabies.

If you have ever visited or thought you would enjoy visiting a national park or just need to commune with nature for a few days to recharge your overworked mental batteries, Hinchinbrook Island will provide a fantastic holiday for you. As they say on their stationery, this friendly resort is *a million miles from the nearest disco.* Such uncrowded and unspoiled natural splendor is too rare.

Hinchinbrook Island Resort
P.O. Box 3
Cardwell, Qld. 4816

[70] 66 8585; telex 148971

Reservations direct to the resort or through Queensland Government Travel Centers

off Hook Island

Hook Island
•unoccupied
•observatory
•scuba diving
•snorkeling
•camping

This is one of the world's most beautiful, essentially unoccupied islands, undeveloped except for the observatory and adjacent facilities on its eastern point. Located opposite Hayman Island to the northwest and almost touching the point of Whitsunday Island to the east, this second largest island in the Whitsunday Group has many of the more important scuba dive and snorkel sites in the region. The *Pinnacle* has excellent corals. The *Woodpile* has a near vertical wall that drops to 110 feet and is definitely not for snorkelers. *Manta Ray Bay* has gullies and tunnels. At the northern end of the island, however, is *Butterfly Bay* where you will find what in our estimation is some of the finest and easiest snorkeling available anywhere for viewing abundant coral and thousands of fish. In addition, if you go ashore, you may see large colonies of *blue tiger butterflies,* with black wings covered with pale blue spots. Look in shaded valleys with dense vegetation.

The air-conditioned observatory with forty viewing windows ($A5 admission and not really that exciting if you are a snorkeler) is situated on a point of Hook Island on a narrow channel separating Hook from Whitsunday Island and is now owned by Ansett Airlines which owns and operates the South Molle and Hayman Island Resorts and brings guests to the observatory regularly from the resort for sightseeing, glass bottom boat trips, or overnight camping. Their boats, however, serve only the jetty at the observatory. To reach the important dive and snorkeling sites, special arrangements must be made to charter a boat or arrange transport by one of the launches from Shute Harbor or from one of the nearby resort islands. The observatory may also be reached from Shute Harbor by day trip via the Hamilton Quick Cat ($A30).

Camping is permitted near the observatory ($A3 per person per day). There is also camping at the south end of the island operated by a company which sells — at substantial   prices — week-long camping vacations with transportation to the island, tents, food with some daily water activities included. Some area residents, while having no objection to individual groups of campers, resent the commercial use of this national park island by these entrepreneurs. There are no tourist accommodations per se on the island other than the showers, toilets, well, beer garden, gift shop and coffee shop maintained by Telford at the observatory.

If you are sailing in the Whitsundays, Hook Island offers the two finest sheltered anchorages in the Whitsunday Passage — *Nara* and *Macono* — on its south coast. These two long narrow inlets surrounded by hills resemble fjords. They are placid and beautiful and often the over-night location for charter boats particularly when weather threatens.

observatory on Hook Island

Some fish nibble the coral polys, while others catch minute worms and other life which live among the corals.

Lady Elliot Island
•coral viewing•national park
•bushwalks•fishing
•scuba diving•anchorage
•tennis•snorkeling
•swimming•camping

Forty miles south of Heron Island and 190 miles north of Brisbane, this island is at the southern-most point of the Great Barrier Reef and is located on the Outer Reef itself approximately 200 miles north of Brisbane. Part of the Bunker Group of islands, it is a true coral cay and is surrounded by coral reefs. In 1866 a kerosene pressure lighthouse was established on the island which is still available for inspection. It is an excellent diving spot where you can see schools of 15 foot manta rays. There is even an old paddle steamer for wreck diving. There is scuba instruction available for beginners. In addition to excellent snorkeling (equipment for rent at the dive shop) and diving opportunities right from the beach, the island has a glass bottomed boat for coral and fish observation.

Access is by air from Bundaberg ($A90 round trip, thirty minute flights). Bundaberg is an hour's flight north of Brisbane ($A90). Due to weight restrictions, personal luggage on the flight over to Lady Elliot is usually restricted to one suitcase (22 pounds) per persons; sleeping bags and pillows can be carried separately. Day trips ($A95) from Bundaberg or Maryborough include round trip air fare, conducted reef walks (subject to tides and winds), glass bottom boat ride and lunch. For sailors, the anchorage is particularly difficult and not recommended for amateurs.

Lady Elliot has virtually no development at all. Accommodations for up to 80 people are in new beachfront cabins ($A89 per person per day, meals included, with private facilities; $A79 without private facilities) and 12 x 12 safari tents ($A69, shared facilities) with raised timber floors covered in seagrass matting, with bunk and double beds with foam mattresses. The resort has bush-type showers and three flush toilets. Meals are served in the central dining room or on the terrace, and there are tropical barbecues on the beach. The staff will also prepare picnic lunches for you. There is an island bar and a small store with a limited selection of food, cosmetics and souvenirs. Rates include use of snorkel equipment, a conducted reef walk (subject to tides and weather), one ride in a glass bottom boat or a fishing trip.

On this island you enjoy the sea, watch the turtles and the frigate birds, snorkel to your heart's content and perhaps learn scuba diving. The resort operation here is new. If all this sounds good, and if you want to have the distinction of having been to the very southern end of the Great Barrier Reef, and if you happen to be visiting the Gold Coast or Sunshine Coast (other very popular resort areas of Australia's east coast), this island could have strong appeal for you.

Lady Elliot Island Holidays Pty Ltd.
Locked Mail Bag No. 6
Bundaberg Post Office, Qld. 4670

telephone [71] 722 322; telex 49731

Lady Musgrave Island

•no resort
•day trips
•coral cay
•atoll lagoon
•snorkeling

This unusual coral cay south of Fairfax Island and north of Lady Elliot Island in the Bunker Group has a perfect atoll lagoon with a deep narrow entrance probably dug or blasted by Japanese fishermen early this century. It is about 30 miles from the coast and possesses a beautiful long circular reef which sweeps away from the islet to the south and loops back to the north to the single deep entrance. The island is noted for its birds and, during the November to March summer season, turtle nesting. It is without accommodations and historically was visited only by serious sailors.

Lady Musgrave Barrier Reef Cruises conducts a day trip aboard the catamaran M.V. Lady Musgrave departing 7:30 a.m. from Bundaberg ($A70, including lunch) for the two and a half hour catamaran trip to Lady Musgrave. There you have lunch and can swim in the lagoon, snorkel in the coral garden, take a trip in the glass bottomed boat, and take island and reef walks with experienced guides. Scuba diving can also be arranged through them. Same day flight connections with Lady Musgrave 7-passenger seaplanes can be arranged from Brisbane ($A298) and Bundaberg ($A135).

Lady Musgrave Barrier Reef Cruises
Tourist Jetty, 1 Quay St.
Bundaberg, Qld. 4670

telephone (71) 72 9011

Lindeman Island

Lindeman Island

•coral viewing •national park
•bushwalks •fishing
•waterskiing •anchorage •tennis
•golf •sailing •snorkeling
•windsurfing •swimming

This is the most southerly and oldest (established 1929) of the resorts grouped fairly closely in the Whitsunday Islands and is near the southern entrance to the Whitsunday Passage. Lindeman is 40 miles northeast of Mackay. The leasehold to the island was purchased in 1905 by one Captain James Adderton, a coastal explorer, who stocked it with sheep. In 1923 a subsequent purchaser converted it for tourist development; in 1974 P & O Australia (which also operates Heron Island to the south) bought the major interest in the leasehold; and in 1987 a Melbourne group, the Four Seasons Hotel chain, took over operation of the resort. Opening at the end of 1987 after some renovation, the revamped hotel continues to operate as a family resort much as before.

Called the *Family Island*, Lindeman is one of the largest resort islands (but not largest resorts) in the Whitsunday Group although considerably smaller than the unoccupied islands of the area — Whitsunday, Hook and even nearby Shaw just to the south. The terrain does provide protection from the prevailing winds. Some of the island's beaches are much less rocky than others in the region, and the views from the hilltops are superb. Lindeman is also fortunate in that it has a ready availability of fresh water. There are scattered bushlands and there is ample bird life. Blue tiger butterflies with blue spotted black wings are found in abundance in *Butterfly Valley*.

are unpredictable it is probably better to anchor either in the bay at the southeast end of the island sheltered by Shaw Island or in Boat Port on the north side facing Pentecost Island, depending upon from which direction the prevailing winds are blowing.

Where to stay

Lindeman Island Resort has traditionally prided itself on its easy going lifestyle. Under P & O's operation, it offered clean simple accommodations with 92 private rooms for up to 362 guests. The resort offered many discount and promotion packages. All apartments have private bath, shower, double beds, seating area, ceiling fans, refrigerator, coffee maker. Laundry facilities are available in each building for the use of all guests.

The resort continues to offer three different types of accommodations, all accommodating up to four adults. *Whitsunday Units* ($A84 per person per night with all meals) and are situated on the beachfront or in elevated blocks with views of Kennedy Sound. Most have excellent views to the south. Uphill units are served by a delightful old fashioned four passenger "inclinator", a cog wheel transport which takes you up the hillside. *Leilani Units* ($A93 per person) overlook the beach. *Seaforth Units* ($A108 per person) replace the old lower priced Tradewinds Units.

What to do

Guests mingle in the hotel's single large dining room with adequate food and two cocktail lounges, one adjacent to the dining room in the central complex and the other next to the pool in the same tiny building used by the dispensary from 3:00 - 3:30. There is a disco a few nights a week, cabaret nights, dancing in the bar most evenings, and live music or entertainment every night. The particularly well stocked island shop seemed a very pleasant, somewhat above average resort store with a very nice staff. There is also a bank agency as well as a snack bar at the resort.

There are eight beaches for guests at Lindeman, as well as access to nearby Seaforth and Shaw Islands. You can play tennis on a court lighted for night play. You can also golf on a very distinctive hilltop 6-hole course split by the light aircraft runway but with exceptional views; Hamilton Island flies golfing guests to Lindeman to enjoy this course. The resort also offered water skiing,   gaffer sailing, sailing instruction, snorkeling (but clearly not the best in the region), fishing, surf ski, water polo and water volley ball, flight seeing, free cruises, catamaran sailing, a small but very attractive swimming pool in a lush tropical setting, cricket, softball, and cruises to other islands.

The island is a national park with twelve miles of scenic nature trails and bush walking.   Near the resort one finds scores of rainbow lorikeets (multicolored parrots).   You can take a pleasant walk to the dam which supplies water for the golf course and the resort.   In the area there are ducks, swamp hens, cormorants, sulphur crested cockatoos and more lorikeets. Kayaks are available for use at the dam.

The resort has always made a special point of catering to families. They offer free group play activities for   children three to eight every morning.   Children's activities include hikes, barbecues, races, sand castle building, treasure hunts, ping pong. Like South Molle a few miles away, the resort staff will care for your children for you while you dine in the evening. For kids over eight, there is a special island summer camp, *Adventure Valley*, where kids live-out pioneer style in a camp settlement for up to three days with qualified adult Adventure Leaders.

Lindeman was always busy, pleasant, and criss-crossed with beautiful walks offering excellent vistas of almost the entire southern Whitsundays. It was to our mind not the best of resorts or the worst of resorts, but it has   its loyal following and was often fully booked. Presumably under its new management, with completely revamped accommodations, it will fulfill this role with even more verve.

Lindeman Island
Lindeman Island, Qld. 4741

For information contact **Four Seasons Hotels**
Suite L   760 West Sixteenth Street
Costa Mesa CA
[800] 654 9153; in California [800] 922 3559

anchored off Lizard Island

Lizard Island
•*coral viewing* •*national park*
•*fishing* •*waterskiing*
•*scuba diving* •*anchorage* •*tennis*
•*golf* •*snorkeling* •*windsurfing*
•*swimming* •*bushwalks*

Visited by princes and prime ministers, movie stars and magnates, Aussies, Americans and Europeans, this is a large (2500 acres) granite island with magnificent beautiful fringing coral situated just a few short miles from the long ribbon reefs which make up the northern Great Barrier. There aren't enough superlatives to describe the island's Blue Lagoon on its south coast. For natural beauty and professionalism of operation, this is a world-class resort.

This resort is by far the most northerly of the Barrier Reef vacation islands, located well within the tropics at only 14@ 40' latitude south of the equator, sixty miles or so northeast of Cooktown and 145 miles north of Cairns well up the Cape York peninsula. Lizard is a granite island close to the Outer Barrier Reef. Because of the way the reef is segmented and broken up, the resort advertises that it is actually a part of the Great Barrier Reef itself although, unlike the coral cays Green, Heron and Lady Elliot to the south, this is not structurally or architecturally precisely so.

The island was named by Captain Cook during charting of the Barrier Reef in 1770, when he noted several monitor lizards (what we call iguanas and the Australians refer to as goanas) over three feet long. This is a high continental island, somewhat barren in patches, with mountains, a few stands of rain forest, some examples of mangrove swamp and other tropical vegetation, and dozens of birds of the region but no indigenous wild game.

Originally this was an aboriginal ceremonial ground. Only adult males visited the island during certain seasons for their religious purposes. The sad story of Captain Watson and his wife Mary Phillips Watson was preserved in her diary and other records on display in the museum at Cooktown. In 1880 he was in the beche de mere or sea cucumber trade, a young son and Chinese servants to go off with his crew to pursue his trade on islands to the north. The Aboriginal natives found the presence of a woman and an uninitiated young man a terrible sacrilege, and when Captain Watson and his men were unexpectedly   detained, natives of the area attacked. One of the servants was killed immediately and carried off. Mrs. Watson, her son, and remaining wounded servant set themselves afloat — the natives were happy to see them depart — in a large tub used for boiling the beche de mere only to die of dehydration just before a tropical rain storm would have provided them with drinking water. Poor Captain Watson returned to find his family destroyed and later, as it is told, died of a broken heart. Remnants of the walls of the Watson house still stand as a reminder of this early attempt to settle the island.

The island has abundant fresh water. Paw paw (papaya) trees, poinsettias, and other tropical flowers and palms grow abundantly. Because this is a national park island, the government regulates strictly what vegetation may be imported even for landscaping the resort, so the facility makes ample use of the many varieties of plants and flowers which exist indiginously.

What makes this a particularly desirable island aside from its fascinating variety of tropical vegetation and varied terrain is that it is surrounded by a superb example of fringing coral reef with some of the *best coral on the entire Barrier Reef.* There are *miles of beaches,* and twenty-four sandy coves. The water around this island is clear, at times startlingly clear. You can see the coral and fish from out of the water, and fishermen sometimes stalk their prey by sight here.

Getting there

Lizard is most easily reached by a fifty minute Air Queensland flight from Cairns ($A214 round trip) daily except Thursday. The flight to Lizard, taking you over dozens and dozens of awesome patches of the Great Barrier Reef itself is the type of sightseeing trip that other resorts offer as a costly extra. There are no day boat trips to Lizard; it is simply too removed from the mainland. Because of the fringing reef, the island has a superb yacht anchorage for those who wish to sail in by themselves, but the resort welcomes yachties only by prior arrangement or invitation.

Air Queensland does offer two different day flights out of Cairns to see Lizard. One ($A220 including flight and buffet lunch) operates Thursday and Sunday and is focused on snorkeling, including a trip to the island's famous "cod hole." The other ($A215) operates daily and includes a brief breakfast visit to Cooktown, a flying tour of the reef at 500', lunch on Lizard and a chance to do a little snorkeling. The *goonies* (so named because they so often come to marvel at Lizard's justly famous Blue Lagoon) are provided with their own special hut — the large Fisherman's Barn at the east end of the resort—with changing rooms and lounge area; if there are less than fifteen in the day trip party, they will lunch at the resort if it is not too fully booked. During marlin season   crews of the charter fishing boats which resort guests have hired eat their meals at the Barn.

Where to stay

At the airport guests are met by the genial staff and driven to the central lodge by small bus. First comes a complementary welcome cocktail and first-name introductions all around. (This theme of informality is a definite part of the motif, going so far as staff members addressing Australia's Prime Minister and his wife by their first names during their visit.) The exceptionally personable staff has been well recruited from all over Queensland, well trained and supervised by resort manager Trish Low, and instructed to make all guests feel completely at home. They specialize in nice touches: a tropical flower by the basin, beds turned down at night, the ice man who comes daily to deliver fresh ice into the storage compartment of your veranda table around 4:00 pm, the pleasant greeting   from all staff people you encounter around the resort.

After your relaxing introduction, you are taken to your bungalow where your luggage already awaits you. As you walk to your room, you will immediately be impressed by the beautiful landscaping, including large expanses of tailored lawn so difficult to maintain in the sandy soil and tropical heat and the variety of flowers around each building, all of this running down to a lovely white sand beach and the sheltered bay.

Lizard Island Lodge ($A270 per person per day, all meals included; two larger *executive units* at $A320; no children under six; children six to twelve half price) is modeled throughout after an Australian pioneer homestead   with a large veranda. The roofs on all the buildings slope upwards from the front to the back of the bungalows providing good ventilation and, with the overhead fans, draining the tropical heat quite nicely. The recently expanded operation has accommodations for sixty-four people (and they firmly say that will be the absolute maximum) in extremely comfortably appointed carpeted bungalow units — two per single story building — overlooking Anchor Bay through glass doors — twenty-four with king bed, six with two oversized double beds, and the two executive suites with king beds and a separate sitting room — all with patios facing beachfront, sofas which can convert to an extra bed, and refrigerators restocked daily with wine, beer, spirits, chocolates, and Lizard Island fruit cake. Each room has the ubiquitous tea/coffee maker as well as an iron and ironing board, air conditioning and overhead fan, a beach umbrella and rain umbrella, large beach towels and beach mats for two. There are no radios, televisions or telephones. Baths are quite attractive with double sinks, hair dryers, a selection of toiletries — replenished daily, and lush oversized bath towels. Unfortunately in a few of the units the bathrooms abut and act as excellent sound conductors to the next bungalow.

The redecorated and carpeted common area, including the elegant dining complex, is in soft whites and pastels like the guest units. An entire wall of windows allows beautiful views of the resort and the bay. To one side of the reception area is the small store with a limited selection of resort wear, sundries and souvenirs as well as the small circulating library. There is an attractive intimate bar for before dinner cocktails and complementary hot hors d'oeuvres each evening. In the dining room and on the large veranda, tables for each meal are set with elegant formal service, and even foods put out on the small buffet are decorated with taste and an appreciation for appearance. Excellent quality very attractive nouveau cuisine meals feature an emphasis on salads, freshly caught reef fish, fresh fruits. The restaurant has in fact won an award as one of Australia's best resort kitchens.

Breakfasts start with a buffet selection of fruit juices, fresh fruits and cold cereals. Hot breakfasts of eggs done any way you wish, omelets, fresh fish, steaks, other meats, pancakes, anything else you might ask for, are readily available. Served lunches offer a choice of fish or meat, always excellent, and you may opt to be served out on the veranda overlooking the bay.

Dinners begin with an excellent imaginative entrée. Main courses for dinner always present at least three selections, one of which will be fish and the other an excellent steak. Some nights the third choice might be fine lamb, roast pork or veal, and one night a week there is a buffet held down at the *Fisherman's Barn* at the end of the resort which can only be described as picturesque. There is a fine selection of wines at middling to higher resort prices ($A18 and up) with a perfectly drinkable inexpensive carafe wine always available ($A8). Fresh coffee at all meals is served in individual French *filtre* pots for each table.

One thing which we appreciated was the fact that you could elect to make meals a very sociable time or, if you felt private and romantic, ask for a table for two. Most often, however, people were so friendly that groups of four and six would form up over cocktails and adjourn to   the dining room to get better acquainted over dinner. Though cordial and charming, service by this well trained staff was at all times impeccable and thoughtful.

What to do

Lizard Island is an international Game Fishing Association weighing station and a base for marlin boats during the game fishing season. It boasts some of the world's outstanding game fishing waters outside of the excellent fringing coral reef. During the October-November season, black marlin often over 1000 lbs are taken. Except for record-breakers, most are tagged and released. During that time the resort is jammed with some of the world's most serious fishermen, and the evening talk at dinner heavily emphasizes the day's catch. Of course, for those who would relish a virtually empty resort and island during daytime while fishing fanatics are at sea and don't mind   the fact that most of the other guests are intent on breaking deep sea fishing records, this would be a good time to visit if you can get reservations.

The annual *Black Marlin Classic* is held here from October 30 to November 5. This is an all tackle tournament run by the Lizard Island Game Fishing Club (membership $A30 per year), formed to cater to anglers based at the resort   and those staying on mother ships or game boats and providing an affiliation with other game fish organizations in Australia and internationally. It is not a money tournament, and the emphasis is on tagging and releasing the giant fish unless they are close to the record catch of 1347 pounds. Halloween is an annual bash with three hundred or more people from the resort and the game fishing boats, with a live band and the festivities *raging* — Australian for   partying — late into the night. The entire week is dedicated to the world's best deep sea fishing.

The resort virtually guarantees that you will hook plenty of fish here any time, and chartering the game fishing boat with its experienced crew almost guarantees non-stop   catches. There are abundant yellowfin tuna (record catch 62 pounds), bonita, sailfish (record 132 pounds), mahi mahi, barracuda (record 64 pounds), spanish mackerel, red emperor (record 27 pounds), grey snapper, and coral trout (record 22 pounds) among dozens of the at least forty-six varieties caught in nearby waters, and the pleasure fishing is excellent year-round. The chef of course is delighted to cook up your catch, and many guests share their good fortune with the other guests of the resort in the form of sashimi or other appetizers or hot lunches. Some Australian guests had their large catch cut into fillets, frozen and packed into coolers which the management permitted them to use to take their prize from resort to home freezer when they departed!

The island features good scuba diving within thirty minutes of the resort to various spots along the Great Barrier Reef with such picturesque names as *Cook's Passage, Dynamite Passage, Shrimp Caves* and *Big Bommie.* In the *Cod Hole,* you can see and pet giant potato cod which live there in thirty foot reef protected waters. The island offers diving instructions and sends guides along on dive trips. There is a daily dive trip ($A85, and weather permitting) which includes tank and weight belt, dive boat and guide. You can rent regulators, gauges, and BCs, and wetsuits. Bring your own photographic gear.

Lizard Island offers some of the best skin diving in the Coral Sea and South Pacific (or even elsewhere in our experience). You can walk right into Anchor Bay towards Prince Charles Island at the left edge of the resort's beach and see angel fish of all colors, butterfly fish, parrot fish, trout, snapper, even an occasional crustacean. The size of these tropical fish is most exciting compared to other island snorkeling. There are also very impressive coral formations with a lot of blue tip staghorn, and *Watson's Bay* adjacent to the Lodge is the home of some of the largest giant clams you will see anywhere with their huge colorful mantels. The resort thoughtfully gives you a map with the best snorkeling areas around the island and its neighbors plainly and accurately marked.

Climb *Cook's Look!*   This is the ridge running across the island adjacent to Watson's Bay and was the peak from which Captain Cook examined the reef for evidence of a passage. The view from the top of this 1167' palisade is absolutely breathtaking. You can see the whole island, the *Blue Lagoon*, the bays, outer islands, the whole Lizard reef structure, and the mainland in the distance. It will take the hardy climbers about forty-five

one Lizard Island's many beaches

minutes and the more relaxed vacationer perhaps two hours in each direction. There is some clambering up granite slabs, so take good ripple-sole or deck shoes for traction. Stop at the reception desk for a canteen full of fresh water before you start out, for the climb can be dehydrating. Once or twice a week the resort guides a group up and down the peak just after dawn and refreshes climbers with champagne.

At the summit, you will find a commemorative stone marker and a brass plaque indicating the distances to various points in the world. Be sure to sign the book stored in the plastic box under the monument at the top, and don't forget to sign in again at the reception desk after your climb. The staff doesn't climb the peak each day to see who has been there.) For your efforts, you will be rewarded not only by the spectacular views but also by a truly handsome certificate awarded by the resort at dinner attesting to your feat.

Take out one of the sturdy five-passenger motor boats. They have new good-sized outboard engines and were among the most substantial dinghies we were offered at any   resort, particularly without extra charge. The resort asks only that you sign out for the boats stating where you are going and when you will return so they can insure that no guests are ever stranded. Except when the winds are particularly strong, these boats will get you most anywhere around the island or even across to Palfrey Island where the lighthouse is situated or to other parts of the Blue Lagoon. Some of the best skin diving in the world is to be found between Palfrey and South Islands, weather permitting.

The *Blue Lagoon*, almost as big in area as the land mass of the island itself, is bounded by the south shore and the sweeping coral reef. Palfrey Island is at the west edge, South Island at the south point of the lagoon, and Bird Islets at the east edge just next to the lagoon entrance. From the shore, you can make out the presence of several subreefs within the bay, while viewed from above the reef activity is nothing short of spectacular. There is an amazing variety of color and depth to the water. This is a must visit, probably more than once during your stay on Lizard.

While you are here, you can fish from the dinghies inside the reef right in the bay in front of the resort if you wish. Other activities include swimming, tennis (rackets and tennis balls free at the reception desk), water skiing, wind surfing, paddle boards, a new swimming pool, archery, and the glass bottom boat. Any time you request, the kitchen will prepare a romantic cold picnic lunch or barbecue for you to take to one of the many secluded beaches or to a nearby island on the fringing reef. You can request your lunch in a cooler, in which case it will be placed in your waiting dinghy at whatever time you specify, or in back packs so you can explore rain forrest or peaks in romantic solitude.

There are two or three pleasant walks through the island national park. We recommend a visit to the *Lizard Island Research Station* around the point from the resort. On Mondays and Thursdays at 4:00 p.m. the staff of the station puts on a slide show and explains their work on the island and adjacent waters. American-born Ph.D. marine biologists Norm Quinn and wife Barbara Kojis run this fascinating facility affiliated with the Australian Museum, Australia's version of the Smithsonian.

Of course, you can also lie around the resort and just relax in the chaises on the elegant lawn overlooking the beautiful beach or by the new pool, but you may find with so many activities available that you have little time left to do just nothing.

It probably wasn't too hard for you to notice our enthusiasm for this island which many people consider their favorite in the Great Barrier

Reef region and beyond. It is not surprising that in 1986 Lizard was named best resort   in Australia and is the first Australian hotel or resort to be nominated for inclusion in the prestigious French *Relais et Chateau*. We certainly didn't mind that the resort doesn't even have a direct telephone line — not   even for the resort itself. Calls must be routed by marine radio-telephone from OTC out of Townsville or by telex through the booking office in Cairns which has a private cable line only with this resort.

Air Queensland was an original part owner of this facility; with Australian Airlines' takeover of that airline, they now become a principle in this resort as well. We sincerely hope they remain the silent partner that Air Queensland has been, for why tamper with such a successful formula?

Due to its location, a trip to Lizard most likely will be the beginning or climax to your sojourn to these island resorts. However, because it is so far off the beaten track (even for Great Barrier Reef hotels), is so popular with fishing parties and has such exclusive accommodations, it is probably wise to invest the $10 or $15 dollars in a direct telephone call to Air Queensland in Cairns or telex the resort directly when you are first planning your Australia itinerary to see whether this pleasant and hospitable island will be able to accept your reservation.

Lizard Island Lodge Pty Ltd.
P.O. Box 2372
Cairns, Qld. 4870
telephone [70] 504 222; telex 48448

Reservations through Air Queensland or Australian Airline

on Long Island

Long Island
**•coral viewing•national park
•bushwalks•fishing•waterskiing
•anchorage•tennis•golf•sailing
•snorkeling•windsurfing•swimming**

Thick undisturbed rain forest covers most of this pretty island. It is one of the larger in the Whitsunday Group and the only island other than Magnetic to the north to have more than one distinct overnight facility. Long is the closest resort island to the coast, visible at night, located just about five miles southeast of Shute Harbor. The island forms a beautiful passage for the coastal sail from Shute Harbor south into the Whitsunday group.

Getting there & Where to stay

Up until just a few years ago, *Happy Bay Resort* toward the northern end of Long Island was a quietly popular family resort, a favorite among many local residents. Then suddenly a new group of entrepreneurs obtained a sublease and converted the resort to *"Whitsunday 100"*, and their brochures announced the resort was "for 18 - 30's" (they don't permit children under 18) and that their swinging scene would make Great Keppel Island seem as tame as a *vicarage tea party*. Based on our inspection we would even lower that upper age range somewhat, but the idea there was clear: *this resort is definitely for the young in mind.* Rumor has it that the resort actually turned away a wealthy Australian notable when he radioed from his yacht for reservations but admitted to being over thirty!

Since our visit the operation has been taken over by Contiki Holidays, an Australia touring company with offices nationwide specializing in packages for the 18-30 age group. Closed for a while for very needed renovation, Contiki has reopened with the same theme.

The resort is reached by daily launch from Shute Harbor ($A23 round trip; about 20 minutes) or connection with flights in and out of Hamilton Island ($A40 round trip; 35 minutes.) Helicopter service is available from Proserpine but must be arranged.

Forty-four budget style *resort cabins* ($A85 per person per night, includes all meals and complementary   carafe of wine with lunch and dinner) face the beachfront. There are blocks of one-story units and some ever-so-slightly-larger free-standing bungalows all rather reminiscent of college dormitory facilities. Units have showers, refrigerators, ceiling fans, tea and coffee making facility, double and day beds, and little else.

What to do

The old dining room and cocktail lounge desperately need a decorator's touch. (Actually, that's true of most   of the resort!) In the reception area, one found the *Ripoff Shop* — honestly, that's what they called it. Nearby there is a barbecue area, a recreation area and dance hall. Activities included wind surfing, catamarans, Aussie 12 yachts (@ scale mini Australia II's), cricket, football, surf skis, snorkeling, water skiing, dinghies, fishing, tennis on an obviously only occasionally maintained compressed clay/sand court, ping pong, and lots of *everyone into the pool for volley ball.*   Room rates include use of all sporting and marine equipment. (Scuba, paraflying, day cruises and reef flights are extra.) There were also lots of signs around telling you how to recover from the "morning after" effects of the night before.

The resort advertised "the best resort beach in the   Whitsunday Passage." Regrettably this beach becomes a swamp at low tide — we left our dinghy too far up on the sand and strained many muscles and all patience getting it back to the water line which quickly retreated as the tide went out.

In defense of *Whitsunday 100* — or to give them equal time, if you will — we give you extracts from a recent brochure: "If the pace doesn't flatten you, a falling coconut probably will." "The island where some people actually manage to do it standing up." "The island where some people prefer to do it sitting down." "The island where there are 3 girls for every boy." "The island where there are 3 boys for every girl." "The island where D.J. means Discovered in the Jungle."

Whitsunday 100 may appeal to you, but more likely it will remind you of the college beer bust that got entirely out of hand. For U.S. visitors travelling all the way to the Great Barrier reef, we frankly believe the idea isn't terribly attractive.

***

A twenty-minute walk south from Whitsunday 100 along a well-marked path brings you to *Palm Bay*, a very small do-it-yourself camp, which bills itself as "the littlest Whitsunday resort." You can also reach Palm Bay directly by launch ($A16 round trip) from Shute Harbor departing at 9:15 a.m. and noon daily. A total of 56 guests may be accommodated in *Lanoo units* ($A66 daily, without meals, for up to six people) or *Koobala units* ($A54 daily, without meals, sleeping up to eight). These are accommodations with minimal amenities. Units have ceiling fans, linen, cutlery, cooking facilities and refrigerators, with communal showers and toilets close by. The island shop, part of the management/reception cabin, is moderately well stocked so you can prepare your own meals. Available activities are water sports, bush walking, fishing, oystering and barbecues, and there is daily ferry service to join up with Whitsunday cruises and yacht trips. Palm Bay is one step above camping and allows you to be in a beautiful part of the world and enjoy the water. And you're far enough from Whitsunday 100 that you may be able to ignore it entirely.

Whitsunday 100
c/o Contiki Holidays Pty. Ltd.
100 Clarence Street
Sydney, NSW 2000

Resort telephone: [79] 469 400

Palm Bay Resort
PMB 28
Mackay, Qld. 4741
telephone [79] 469 233
Reservations direct to the resort

A school of fish just below the surface of the water

Low Islets

•no resort
•day trips
•densely forested
•coral atolls

Every day at 10:00 the Reef Express leaves Port Douglas Wharf for the brief trip to the Low Islets. Theze tiny yet densely forested coral atolls have long been a favorite day trip of those familiar with the Barrier Reef. The only permanent residents of this tiny isle are the lighthouse keepers and their families, and there are no overnight hotel or resort facilities. What makes this trip a favorite is the close proximity to major portions of the Barrier Reef, allowing some of the best snorkeling and coral viewing in northern Queensland. There is also a glass bottom boat, but those with rubber shoes can generally walk right from the beach onto at least part of the reef, weather and tides permitting.

The day trip ($A40 per person, or $A48 including round trip bus service from Cairns) includes smorgasbord luncheon, morning and afternoon tea and snack, and the use of snorkel gear and the glass bottom boat. If by any chance you have kitchen facilities available where you are staying, you might be interested in joining the locals buying fresh fish from the fishing boats that sell part of their daily catch to the lighthouse keepers and their families — and to the day visitors to Low Islets.

The boat returns to Port Douglas at 4:30 p.m. in plenty of time to permit easy return to Cairns in ample time for dinner.

For further information or advance reservations contact Maritime World, 2618 Newport Blvd., Newport Beach, California 92663; telephone [714] 675-2250 or Cairns Tour Service [070] 51 8311.

Tuesday lawn bowling on Magnetic Island

Magnetic Island

Magnetic Island
•coral viewing•national park
•bushwalks•fishing•scuba diving
•anchorage•tennis •golf•sailing
•snorkeling•windsurfing
•swimming•horseback riding

Named by Captain Cook in 1770 because his compass appeared to be influenced by the island while the *Endeavor* was near it, in fact the island is *not magnetic* although it does possess substantial deposits of the mineral magnetite which will affect the old astrolabe compass. This rather dry hilly and rocky island is roughly three miles wide and twelve long. Seventy percent of the island is national park and bird sanctuary. There are several very pleasant bays, particular the very photogenic *Arthur Bay,* with interesting rock formations. There are also indigenous koala, rock wallabies and numerous birds. The national park has several well graded walking trails.

Getting there

Like Green Island, Magnetic was first served in 1899 by the Butler family who started the ferry service which later became Hayles. This is a fairly large continental island and is the biggest of the northern islands. It is in reality not a resort island but an island of resorts as well as being a suburb of Townsville, just five miles off coast, where about 2500 people live and as many as 600 commute daily to the City. Reached by Hayles Cruises ferries or the new Westmark launch services ($A7.50 round trip) — both operating roughly every hour during daylight — or the three-times-a-day Hayles vehicle ferry ($A60 round trip for one car and two adults), you can also fly in via Rundle Air Service or helicopter from Townsville. You can sail to Magnetic — the anchorage is at Picnic Bay at the   south end — but it is a poor location for overnight mooring, and the channel can get a bit rough during bad weather periods.

The several village-like areas are linked by roads with bus and taxi service available. The main road runs from Picnic Bay at the south end of the island to Horseshoe Bay on the northern end. There is a network of paved roads branching from the main road around the settlements at Picnic Bay, Nelly Bay and Arcadia as well as the old paved road past Arthur Bay to Radical Bay where there is another resort. The eastern shoreline is developed; the rest of the island is readily accessible wilderness. In all there are five populated bays with tourist facilities.

Where to stay

Accommodations range from hotel/motel units to self-contained flats. These resorts, unlike much of the Barrier Reef area, are part of developed free hold properties and are not on lease. There are hotels, holiday resorts, numerous motels, guest houses, holiday flats, hostels, and camping areas. Westmark, a Western Australia resort and leisure corporation, operates *Latitude 19* located inland from Nelly Bay. Tell them which ferry you will be on when you make your reservation, and they will pick you up at the landing. This attractive resort — largest on the island — has eighty-two *Lodge units* ($A75) and sixteen *Executive Suites* ($A90). Rooms have showers, air conditioning as well as overhead fans, TV and radio, piped music, touch tone telephones, tea and coffee maker and refrigerator. The suites are larger and feature a separate bedroom with a lounge and dining area. The hotel has also added sixteen *Deluxe Suites* ($A100) which are slightly larger and, situated further up the slope, have decks with views of Townsville. There is an attractive cocktail lounge and a friendly restaurant; in the evenings the resort features a delightful two-man band which plays literally everything! The attractive pool area is just below the restaurants, allowing pleasant dining on the restaurant terrace overlooking the pool and the resort, and the two carpet tennis courts are just to the side. There are koalas, possums and kookaburras wild on the grounds.

Hayles operates the refurbished and expanded *Arcadia Holiday Resort* which also will send a car to the landing for you on your arrival. At the Arcadia there are *Poolside* ($A65), *Terrace* ($A75) and *VIP Suite* ($A90) rooms, all with air conditioning, color TV, telephones and the usual coffee maker. The resort has snack shops, a coffee shop, boutiques, a small post office, laundry facilities and *Skipper's* restaurant, two bars, convention facilities, snack bars, and two large terraced swimming pools — biggest on Magnetic Island — overlooking nearby Arcadia Bay. There are darts and pool tables in the lounge. On Wednesday evenings there are toad races, and there is a variety of evening entertainment in *Skippers'*, the *Beer Garden* and the *Terrace Lounge*. The Arcadia offers a *standby rate* ($A59 per person) which includes dinner, breakfast and the round trip launch from Townsville. The *Magnetic Hotel* has *Lodge* ($A45) and *Budget* ($A35) rooms.

A controversial new resort development has been approved for Nellie Bay over the protests of many residents of Magnetic Island. The "fancier" — all very informal — restaurants are at the resorts. In all there are a dozen licensed restaurants and several bars and cafes. The best food, however, is found at the small *BYOs* around the island. At dinnertime *Maggie's Restaurant*, the informal *Esplanade* lunch place at Picnic Bay, turns into one of the island's   finest. Try the fresh-baked flat bread and also the chunks of camembert cheese deep fried in a filo dough wrapper as an appetizer! The bugs with a cheese sauce were excellent as was the fresh — but more expensive, sold according to market price — mud crab with a reisling sauce. The excellent food was enhanced by the quality of the service, with even the wine service — from your own stock — handled elegantly, yet prices were very moderate. As an additional bonus you also get a great view of the lights of Townsville across the channel.

For very fresh fish, try *Banister's*. Open until 8:00 pm, this charming take-out shop is really the island fish market, situated next to the what the Arcadia settlement generously refers to as its *shopping center* around the corner from the main road. There are four or five picnic- type tables in front for the lunch traffic. Here the fresh catch is listed on the blackboard, and fish and chips is priced by the piece of fish depending upon what type you specify. Fresh prawns, lobster, bugs and crayfish — depending upon the catch — are also offered. In the fridge you will find salads and soft drinks; for wine or beer, you can stop at the bottle shop at the Arcadia Resort around the corner.

For a dinner treat when you are in a mood for Italian food, try *alla Capri* (a licensed restaurant) on Hayles Road also in the Arcadia area. The pizza was particularly good.   Magnetic Island boasts that you can enjoy any activity offered at any other barrier reef resort all on one island. There is swimming either in your hotel pool or at one of the many beaches. Be careful in the summer, since Magnetic is close to river estuaries and is very prone to the box jellyfish during that season. There is a net across Picnic Bay and one being installed at Radical Bay to allow free use of the beaches during summer months without worry. There are occasional shark alerts, so check with your hotel staff to see if there is any peril while you are visiting.

What to do

Many people rent mini-mokes (around $A25 per day) or motorbikes from any one of several agencies around the island and sightsee and picnic wherever they wish. There are many very attractive walks, and some hardy souls bicycle around the island up and down the rather steep hills. You can book fishing trips, excursions, trips to the Great Barrier Reef forty miles distant, join the nice people at the lawn bowling club, go horseback riding, golf at the country club ($A4), water ski, rent sail boards or a small catamaran, visit Shark World or just be lazy. At Horseshoe Bay, you can visit the *Oasis Koala Park* ($A4 per person) where injured koalas are cared for and are very approachable; otherwise this is not a particularly interesting zoo.

Day and longer trips can also be arranged directly from Magnetic Island. For example, the Reef Link out of Townsville stops here to pick up and deliver passengers for its day trips to the John Brewer reef and Palm Islands. In addition, Westmark which owns and operates the Latitude 19 resort and ferry service to Townsville is also introducing coastal cruises aboard their M.V. Louisanda carrying up to 32 passengers.

For further information contact the Queensland Tourist and Travel Corp., 611 N. Larchmont, Los Angeles, California 90004; telephone [213] 465-8418

Latitude 19 Resort
Mandalay Avenue
Nelly Bay
Magnetic Island, Queensland 4816

telephone [077] 78 5200; telex 47000

Arcadia Holiday Resort
P.O. Box 411
Townsville, Queensland 4810

telephone [077] 78 5177; telex 47275

Alma Bay—Magnetic Island

Koala bears in captivity on Magnetic Island

Newry Island
•cabins for campers
•fishing
•oystering
•koala santuary

Located 34 miles north of Mackay, Newry is south of Brampton and in a peripheral and rather remote sense part of the Whitsunday Passage group of islands. It is reached by a pick-up boat which leaves from Victor Creek, Seaforth near Mackay ($A10 round trip), at 11:00 a.m. and 4:00 p.m. for the fifteen minute trip. A heavily wooded national park, this 18 acre island boasts excellent fishing and a particularly abundant supply of oysters. It also has a koala sanctuary.

There is a very small unpretentious facility consisting of self-contained cabins for twenty-five guests with little in the way of services but a comparably low price ($A50 per person per day, double occupancy, full board; $A20 per person room only). Units sleep a maximum of five people, and most have cooking facilities. Seafoods caught in the area are the main feature of the dining room dinner menu.

Fishing and oystering are the most popular activities and there is some water skiing. There is no night life, but there is a fully licensed bar open all hours, with meals and snacks available, and darts, pool, and table tennis for guests. For further information telephone [79] 590 214

sunset on Orpheus Island

Orpheus Island
•coral viewing •national park •bushwalks •fishing •waterskiing •scuba diving •tennis •golf •sailing •snorkeling •windsurfing •swimming

This is a relatively long, narrow island, about six miles by 1/2 mile and largely a national park, and is located roughly 50 miles northeast of Townsville. Part of the Palm Islands group, it is 15 miles off shore and within sight of the mainland, near Hinchinbrook Channel, and six or seven miles south of the southern end of Hinchinbrook Island. Orpheus is about nine miles from the outer Barrier Reef. It was named in 1887 by a British Admiralty surveyor to commemorate a ship wrecked two decades earlier off New Zealand with the loss of all hands including the commander-in- chief of the Australia Station.

As with many other islands along the Great Barrier Reef chain, provisions were placed for lost or shipwrecked mariners. Today 400 wild goats still survive as part of this history. There are also remnants of stone sheep pens dating back to early in the century. The island has been used for commercial oystering as well. At the south end of Hazard Bay, south of the beach occupied by the resort, cement pilings remain from a degaussing or demagnetizing station used for submarines during World War II (and also mark the best snorkeling beach on the island). The present ownership bought the island in 1980 and, after two years of planning and complete renovation, opened the resort just before Christmas in 1981.

Geographically the island presents different faces. Volcanic in origin, parts appear relatively dry, while around the next point you will find a lush beach interrupted with a stand of mangrove trees. There are numerous points around the island with large boulders scattered interestingly, and there are abundant pisonia and palm trees. Beaches are generally sandy, although in some areas the inshore coral has died, leaving exposed flats at very low tides. The beaches are relatively shallow, however, and taper nicely into the lagoon, so they are among the best in the tropics for swimming and splashing around, water sports and easy snorkeling.

Getting there

Orpheus is most usually reached by Reef World (formerly Air Whitsunday) 13-passenger seaplane service aboard Grumman twin engine high wing aircraft Wednesday and Saturday from Cairns ($A116 each way) and daily except Tuesday and Thursdays from Townsville ($A82). Interestingly, because Hinchinbrook Island is so close to the north, these flights also serve that island, giving these two barrier reef island resorts the almost unique distinction of being linked directly by air — which might be important if you have travelled eight thousand miles for a holiday and would appreciate some convenience in getting from one resort to another   instead of having to return to the mainland.   There is also available a very expensive helicopter charter (approximately $A500 each way) carrying a maximum of four passengers. Like one couple we were told about, you could charter a plane to pick you up in Cairns at your convenience and deposit you directly in the waters off Orpheus for a mere $A3000 or so; evidently the wife found the guest population too *small* — at the time the resort was somewhat shy of its maximum guest population of fifty, so the couple departed after one night.

There are also launches from Townsville or Dungeness near Ingham or from Lucinda Point on the coast opposite, but prices are high because of the small numbers of people making the passage, and the real problem of getting transportation to Lucinda discourages most people. For now, access is realistically through Cairns and Townsville. There is no deep anchorage available close to shore for boats because of the shallow low tides. Indeed even the resort must moor its larger boats well away from the beach.   In addition, to insure the privacy of the guests and maintain the level of the operation, management discourages visits from yachties without special prior arrangements.

Where to stay

We found this to be a very sophisticated and elegant resort, particularly for such a small independent operation. It is a hideaway for adults, and families with children are only occasionally accepted on a very selective basis. Currently *Orpheus* is managed by Gary Low, formerly at Lizard Island. The style is definitely upscale and intimate. The island lodge accommodates but twenty-five couples — families with children accepted only by special arrangement with management — in recently thoroughly renovated and redecorated rooms. The open-air lounge is beautifully tropical with high ceiling, open sides to allow the tropical breezes to flow through, well situated   to take advantage of the view of ocean and distant coastline, an elegant blend of tropical wood, rattan and blue fabric. "Tea" (that is, coffee and tea and, in the afternoon, sweet   cookies) is served British fashion at eleven and four. The room has an elegant comfort and openness about it. Similarly, the adjacent dining commons is open on three sides, has many overhead fans, and a large attractive and well maintained tropical fish tank for decoration. It is   elegantly yet very simply appointed. Drinks are served on silver trays by what the British would undoubtedly call "a properly attired barman."

There are two types of *studios* ($A207 per person per day, all meals included) grouped four to a building in single story beachfront buildings set inconspicuously into their surroundings. These handsome accommodations, some done in wood and stucco with white tile floors and the others in more Mediterranean style with white stucco and mixed sand and white floor tiles, have double bed and day sofa with ample space for bed and sitting area cooled by an overhead fan, spacious tile shower and separate vanity area, refrigerator with mini bar, tea and coffee-making facilities and a sound system to bring you local radio stations and music. Decor is bright tropical. There are two *bungalow units* ($A227 per person per day) which are luxurious larger detached beachfront units, have queen size beds without a day bed but with a lovely conversation area. Floors are large squares of terra cotta tile. Rooms have ample windows, french doors, potted green plants. Grass cloth walls, a wall of polished dark wood strips set on the diagonal behind the bed, yellow-orange drapes. Handsome wood and rattan furniture. The special feature of the bungalows is a large beautifully appointed tiled "tropical garden bathroom" [that means french doors open onto a tiny private garden outside the window] with extravagant four-foot diameter sunken bath tub with shower.

Up the hill beyond the resort are luxury villas which, we understand, may be available for rental by special arrangement.

The resort provides luxury soaps, face creams, bath oils, extra towels for the beach and at poolside without your asking, and such necessities as a sewing kit, shower cap, insect repellant, hand laundry cream soap, and so forth in the generously supplied apartment. They even give you free copies of the fine waterproof edition of the pamphlet *Introductory Guide to Life on the Great Barrier Reef* published by the Great Barrier Reef

Marine Park Authority. This ingenious publication is designed so you can actually take it underwater while you are snorkeling to compare photos with the real marine world and read brief explanations about what you are seeing.

"Fine tropical dining," said one travel brochure. We'll go further: for a tropical resort, especially one with such a small clientele (remember they can only accommodate fifty people), the resort has a gifted kitchen which we learned had just been placed in the hands of the gentleman who had been working as the under-chef. All three meals are a la carte and served.

Breakfasts are English style and far too generous for most of us: fish, meats, omelets, eggs, fruits, cereals, etc., etc., etc. For lunch and dinner, two or three selections will be offered, depending upon the number of guests at the resort. Generally the choice will be a local fish or a meat or fowl dish. Sauces are offered with the advice that you can ask for any variation you may desire; the chef is quite willing to prepare food to your taste. The wine list is of good quality but with an emphasis on the higher price selections. It is a tad more abbreviated than one might hope for, but this is perhaps understandable given the difficulties of warehousing wines in the tropics, the small number of consumers, and the level of quality the resort obviously strives to maintain. The house wines served from the bar are quite pleasant, can be ordered by glass or carafe, and just as important, both red and white house wines were correctly cared for so they did not become stale and oxidized from the heat.

Dinner was always exciting. Prawns steamed perfectly with an exquisite spicy chili sauce were offered as an entrée (remember again, entrée means introductory course in Australia) but on this evening the dish made a perfect main course for a hot summer evening — one which prompted us to ask for the recipe. For a simpler meal, a filet done exactly as ordered, tender as the finest U.S. beef, served with a bouqueterie of perfectly cooked fresh vegetables with a light butter sauce. Another evening's barramundi (an Australian coastal river fish, generally considered their finest) was superb. The fried scallops with a lemon butter sauce were simple and excellent, just as you might expect in San Francisco or New York. The emphasis throughout is on fresh local foods including tropical fruits and seafood.

Lunches are equally appropriate and properly handled. Cold soup or entrée and fish or meat, followed by a small pleasant fruit and cheese table was the menu for one day. The resort also proudly features its picnic lunches for you to take wherever you might desire on this small island. At the specified time, a large cooler chest is loaded aboard a small motor boat, and you may select your own spot for a totally intimate picnic on a secluded beach. Or, should you prefer to be chauffeured, one of the staff will deposit you by boat on your secluded paradise and pick you up at the appointed hour.

The staff is well coached and very pleasant. Service is attentive and pleasantly but not offensively professional. Unfortunately this island, as with all of the smaller vacation resorts, experiences a fairly high turnover of staff. Thus, the continuation of the high standards depends upon competent management in the training of personnel as they are added, and Orpheus definitely seems to have that. It is evident here that every effort is made to set and maintain an elegant level of polite service.

What to do

The resort has one nicely maintained astroturf tennis court which they service weekly to keep in good shape. They also have a lovely small swimming pool with ocean view, "spa" (hot tub, that is) which seemed amusing to us during the ninety degree heat which lasted throughout our stay. Catamaran, sailing, wind surfing, paddle boards, outboard powered dinghies, snorkeling equipment, and glass bottom viewing boat are all included in price. This relatively small island has seven secluded bays and beaches. For fees quite comparable to those on other islands you can cruise to the Outer Reef (always weather and tides permitting), take fishing trips, charter a speedboat with a driver, or cruise aboard the 30' ketch *Freckled Duck* or 40' cruiser *Orpheus*.

Orpheus Island boasts some of the best coral in the entire Barrier Reef region. The surrounding waters are so rich in marine life that James Cook University has established a Marine Research Station in a quiet area of the island. Like other Barrier Reef islands, Orpheus is also well known for its abundant supply of birds — at least 50 species having been identified.

If the tide is low, the staff urge you to take a motorboat or catamaran and sail to their float in the middle of their peaceful bay from which the snorkeling is excellent right in front of the resort, or to try the bay two beaches to the south where there is abundant live coral near the pilings marking the old submarine mooring spot. If you are planning an

on Orpheus Island

afternoon of swimming, sunning or snorkeling on the float, ask the office for the portable two-way radio to take to the raft; should you become thirsty, you need only call the bar, and the barman will promptly deliver your beverage order by motorboat to the float.

Dress is casual, although the resort invites you to dress up if you wish — and you may find the surroundings so elegant that you will want to. The brochure in your room advises that "we do ask that swimsuits be the minimum dress. For those who wish to get an all over tan, we'll be happy to take you to one of our secluded beaches." There is a tiny boutique which also sells toiletries as well as souvenirs. Commercial laundry service is available. There is only one telephone line to the island, so guests are requested to keep calls to three minutes and can only use the telephone during office hours. Also the staff will book your on-going Air Whitsunday flights for you, and you can add them to your bill to enable you to put them on a credit card if you are not already ticketed.

Orpheus is where Australian movie stars and visiting British nobility go to relax in the tropics. It is an island for couples who enjoy being alone together, and the resort sets a tone not found on other Barrier Reef islands. This is by no means an inexpensive island, although when you consider all of the activities and amenities included in the price, the load is lightened somewhat. In reality, Orpheus can cost you half-again as much as other resorts. Indeed Orpheus does bill itself as "The Exclusive Barrier Reef Resort," but then again it may be that you are ready for some totally rewarding self indulgence.

Orpheus Island Resort
Private Mail Bag
Ingham, Qld. 4850
telephone [77] 777 377; telex 47434 REEFIS

Reservations direct to the resort or Pacific Insight Marketing, 2618 Newport Blvd., Newport Beach, California 92663; telephone [714] 675-2250 or, from within California, [800] 282-1402; outside of California [800] 282-1401

Palm Island
•aborigine reservation
—permission needed

Located thirty-six miles northwest of Townsville, this continental island is the largest in the Palm group. It was named by Captain Cook who landed there and found it was then inhabited by a tribe of native Australians. In 1918 the Australian government established a *mission or reservation for Aborigines.* The island is governed by an indigenous council and is financed and administered by the Department of Aboriginal and Island Advancement. The population is about 1300.

Except for Orpheus Island just to the north, all islands in the Palm group are part of the Aboriginal reserve and cannot be visited without special permission from the governmental agency administering the mission. Contact must first be made with officials in Brisbane or Townsville or directly with the island manager to obtain permission to use the landing strip or the island. The Reef Link day trip from Townsville offers occasional trips sailing around the Palm Islands group, visiting the Orpheus Island National Park as well, but not stopping at Palm.

Fantome Island in this group was a leper colony until 1974. All of the buildings were then razed by fire and the remaining inhabitants removed to a hospital on Palm Island.

Raine Island
•*no tourist facilities*
•*sea turtle rookery*

Situated off Cape Grenville north of Lizard Island, this is the world's largest rookery. It is the most seaward of the vegetated coral cays. Between November and February as many as 16,000 turtles crowd the island to lay eggs.

There are, however, no tourist facilities on the island.

on South Molle Island

South Molle Island
•coral viewing•national park
•bushwalks•fishing•waterskiing
•scuba diving•anchorage
•tennis•golf•sailing•snorkeling
•windsurfing•swimming

North Molle is for camping, West Molle is better known as Daydream, and there is no East Molle. South Molle, in the middle of Whitsunday Passage roughly sixty miles north of Mackay and five miles from Shute Harbor, until late-1984 was the largest island resort of the Whitsunday Group when it was outstripped by both Hamilton and Hayman Islands. Hilly, covered with grassland, native trees and pockets of rain forest, this national park island is fringed with palm trees, with a coast punctuated with numerous bays, inlets and coral gardens, surrounded by fringing coral reefs. There are bush walks with panoramic views from *Mt. Jeffreys* and *Spion Kop*. There is abundant bird life, and the lorikeets (small multicolored parrots) are fed daily next to the tennis courts. South Molle is one of the most scenic in the Whitsundays, a large island with good walking paths and good hilltop views across the Whitsunday Passage overlooking Hayman, Hook and Whitsunday Islands, among others.

Getting there

The giant high-speed South Molle catamaran carries guests to the resort three times daily from Shute Harbor (A$10 each way) or from the jet airstrip at Hamilton Island daily at various times, meeting the in-coming Ansett flight from Melbourne, Sydney and Brisbane. There are ten boat moorings for visiting yachts ($A20 per day).

Where to stay

South Molle Island Resort is a village style collection of bungalows and multi-unit buildings set in tropical gardens overlooking Bauer Bay. It features a casual, relaxed atmosphere, and its activities are centered around a newly remodeled pool complex. There are currently three categories of accommodations totalling 202 rooms. Units are generally wood paneled and not particularly extravagant or luxury accommodations by U.S. standards. They are somewhat small and old fashioned in style but very clean and equipped with ample amenities.

Whitsunday units ($A150 per person per day, double occupancy, including all meals) are on the beach right in front of the resort and have queen size and single beds, bath tubs as well as showers and telephones. The *Reef units* ($A125) are motel style rooms in back of the Whitsunday group. These pleasant rooms face the golf course rather than the beach and are simpler than the others. There are fifteen Reef units divided for family use with a pull partition to divide the room in two, with singles and bunks for four children. Some of the reef units are uphill, perhaps 200 yards from the main complex, and have a lovely northern view of the bay and, except for bath tubs and tile floors, similar appointments to the Whitsunday rooms. *Beachcomber units* ($A115) are also on the beach front but rather more modest. All apartments have ceiling fans and air conditioning, color television, refrigerators, tea and coffee makers and private balconies.

Like many other Whitsunday area resorts, South Molle offers a considerably reduced stand-by rate for guests reserving less than 48 hours before their arrival and accepting accommodation on an as available basis.

Meals are served in a large rather uninteresting air-conditioned dining area, done in bamboo wood and green plastic, located at the base of the U-shaped complex surrounding the large swimming pool. Lunch is a routine self-service buffet. The kitchen shows little inspiration. Fortunately there is a pianist who plays nightly during dinner. The Friday night buffet dinner does stand out; it is a vast spread which, among other dishes, includes a huge offering of fresh regional fish and shell fish. This highly regarded smorgasbord is touted throughout the Whitsunday area. The South Molle ferry runs a special *booze cruise* on Fridays (the *Island Feast Night cruise*, $A30 all inclusive) to take people from Shute Harbor to South Molle for dinner, remaining for the "south seas" cabaret, and returning via a sweeping tour of the north-central Whitsunday Passage around midnight.

The *Discovery Bar* entertainment center is a vast dark barn of a room filled with cocktail tables and plastic chairs. This cavern triples as a

off South Molle Island

conference center, game room, and evening bar/cabaret to showcase the resident band. It does boast two very large murals by a local artist, one of Captain Cook and the other of his ship the *Endeavor*. Regrettably, the lighting was so poor in the room that the murals are probably only noticed by ten percent or less of the visitors to the resort.

What to do

Evening activities, aside from the resident band, include discos, dress-up frolics, amateur nights, bingo, and toad and crab racing. As indicated earlier, most all of the rooms have television, and there is a large screen TV in the game room section of the entertainment center. There are coin-operated laundry facilities, banking and postal office, high chairs and cots for children, an island photographer. The island store was, in our estimation, significantly understocked for a resort of this size. The small arcade of shops includes a small diving store, hair-dresser, laundry, and snack bar.

South Molle possesses a beautiful nine-hole golf course and has a resident professional. Clubs are $A3 for half day rental, and balls and tees are available for purchase. There are two paved all-weather tennis courts with lights for night playing, and there is no charge for court time. (Tennis rackets, however, are $A2.50 per hour!) There is a squash court (rackets $A1.50 per half hour), free archery, a gymnasium with spa and sauna, volleyball, ping pong, badminton, lawn bowling, billiards, pin ball machines, beach cricket and softball games. There are also separate programs for children, including wading pool, playground, game room and the like.

Children are supervised free of charge in the nursery from 6:00 p.m. to 9:00 p.m. nightly to permit parents to have dinner alone; otherwise, baby sitting is provided by off-duty hotel staff at normal rates.

The water sports are ample, and free equipment is available for paddle skiing and snorkeling, water bicycles and wind surfers. The resort also offers parasailing ($A20 per ride, also including instruction), water skiing ($A6 without instruction, $A10 with), and dinghies with five horsepower motors ($A10 per hour). Scuba instruction ($A45 for an introductory course; $A250 for the full five day PADI accredited course) is available. You can fish off the jetty ($A2 to rent a fishing rod, $A1 for a hand line) and you can buy bait.

There are day and half-day cruises visiting Daydream, Hayman, Long, Lindeman, Dent, or Hamilton among other destinations (beginning at $A20). Weather and tides permitting, there are day cruises to the outer reef ($A50 to $A90). The resort owns a float and a moored submarine at the outer reef permitting visitors to get a real close-up view. Scuba equipment is available for rent ($A25). The resort runs nearby boat trips for diving ($A25 per person for scuba or snorkelers) and outer reef dive trips ($A40 per person).

This resort is owned by the Ansett Airlines which just took over from the Telford Hotel chain, an Australian operation with resorts and hotels across the country. Ansett also purchased the observatory at Hook Island (admission $A5), so for the non-snorkeler or other fan of underwater viewing rooms there are frequent trips to Hook Island. For a while the Telford chain was in an Australian form of receivership, and its properties were being operated by trustees. Little was done to upgrade South Molle during that period. Now that Ansett has taken over, South Molle has been refocused to take over the role formerly served by

Hayman Island before the massive upgrading of that nearby Whitsunday area resort. The emphasis at South Molle is on families, and promotional materials emphasize the ease of having additional people in the rooms. The resort does continue to enjoy a fine reputation in its own right.

South Molle may not offer the most exciting rooms or food, but it does have one of the most complete activities   programs for a resort of its size. Many long-time residents of the Whitsunday area rank this resort very high on their list.

South Molle Island Resort
Post Mail Box 21
Mackay, Qld 4741

telephone [79] 469 433; telex 48132

South Molle Travel Centre
43 Shute Harbor Road
Airlie Beach

telephone [79] 466 900

Reservations through Ansett Airlines

View of Whitsunday Passage

Whitsunday Island
•national park
•no resort
•beach camping

This very large island national park, biggest of the islands in the group to which it gives its name, is the center of a group of resort and uninhabited islands off Proserpine, about midway along the Queensland coast. Captain Cook landed here in 1770, naming the island for the day on which he set foot there. Markers at Cid Harbor on the west coast of the island commemorate the landing.

Whitsunday Island has no resort although camping is permitted on the island at several beach points. The island itself is too densely forested to permit much interior trekking except by the hardiest explorer. Cid Harbor offers a good anchorage to sail and power boats as well as a very pretty beach. By small boat you can reach some smaller even prettier beaches just around the bend to the north of Cid. On the southeast side of the island, Turtle Bay is a particularly interesting and attractive anchorage.

The Whitsunday Passage separates the islands of the Whitsunday group —Hook, Whitsunday, Border, Haslewood, Hamilton, Dent and Cid— from the main land. Daydream, South Molle, Pine and Long Islands lie offshore. There are seventy-four islands within the Whitsunday and (just to the south) Cumberland groups, many virtually uninhabited. Day cruises are available to Whitehaven Beach from Shute Harbor ($A30) and from Hamilton Island ($A12) on board the *Hamilton Quick Cat*, a large modern high-speed catamaran.

The resort islands arrayed to the north, west and south (no resorts to the east) around Whitsunday are (counter-clockwise from the north) Hayman, Daydream, South Molle, Long (Whitsunday 100 and Palm Bay camping cabins), Hamilton and Lindeman. The underwater observatory on Hook Island (owned and operated by Ansett) is just across the narrow channel separating northern Whitsunday from Hook. If you are in the Whitsunday Passage, Hook Island is particularly worth a visit even though it has no resort, because it offers the best scuba diving and snorkeling in the area.

Cairns

Brisbane—Queensland state capitol

Coastal Cities and Towns

The North Queensland coastline is itself a growing vacation land. All of the cities and towns along the way are now advertising resorts, and indeed many of them show great promise. This is an old and fiercely independent part of Australia — but then again, so is much of the continent, but people here live much as they did fifty years ago. Since you inevitably must spend at least some time in and around gateway cities (and the airports are generally but a few minutes' taxi ride from the center of town), we thought some information about them and their sister towns would be interesting.

BRISBANE

Brisbane ("BRIZ-bn" to locals) calls itself the Gateway City, and for many it is the first stop in the northerly tour to the Great Barrier Reef or the climax of the southerly journey through Queensland. Geographically this capitol of the State of Queensland is the third largest city in the world, incorporating a huge area within a single city limits although its population is just under a million making it Australia's third city. An international port for Qantas, with service by both national jet airlines and several feeder carriers, and with regular bus and rail traffic, the city is favored by temperate climate virtually throughout the year and so is base city for the nearby Gold Coast forty-five minutes to the south and less developed but increasingly popular, Sunshine Coast one hour to the north.

Taxi fare in from the airport should be under $A10, and the trip ordinarily is only twenty minutes or so unless at rush hour or when the roads are congested for some other reason. If you find yourself in Brisbane for a day or so, the downtown area is very compact, easily toured on foot, and is definitely cosmopolitan with a colorful mix of modern highrise interspersed with old small brightly-painted Victorian and Edwardian buildings. A two block strip of Queen Street in the main shopping area has been closed to vehicle traffic to form a delightful mall (here pronounced like the "a" in "pal"). At either end there are outdoor restaurants (both called *Jimmy's At the Mall)* at one end serving fish dishes and at the other meat and diverse snack lunches. The *Brisbane Visitors Bureau* is situated in a kiosk at the Albert Street end of the mall, and people there are very graciously helpful with shopping, restaurant, touring and other advice for travellers.

The City Hall on King George Square, just a block from the mall, is a dramatic stone building with its marble interior and tall clock tower and a fine example of Edwardian civic architecture. Behind the City Hall is a small square with several shops (including a large news agency) and restaurants; we particularly enjoyed *Agatha Christie's* — an elegant recreation of an Orient Express dining car—it is open for lunch and dinner. The Barrier Reef is an excellent fully licensed seafood restaurant on Albert Street a block from the mall.

Incidentally, although not known by many airline staffers or even many locals, we found that you can check things until 10:00 p.m. for 45 cents at the cloak room in the ladies' lounge in the side basement of the City Hall with its separate entrance on Adelaide Street. This is very convenient if you find yourself with a long day between flights or otherwise want to park your bags, especially since only the domestic air terminal in Brisbane has lockers. The international terminal where Qantas lands does not.

The brief tour of Brisbane should include the short walk down George, Albert or Edward Streets to Alice Street to see the attractive *Botanic Gardens*. With the interesting *Parliament House* and other public buildings nearby and with its pleasant tailored grounds, this is a most handsome public city park. Bicycles may be rented on Margaret Street near the Parkroyal Hotel for riding in the Gardens, and there are snack trucks near the bandstand area. The Gardens are bordered on three sides by the Brisbane River, and the river bank is a pleasant setting for just watching the boats or perhaps a picnic. The Edward Street ferry runs from the edge of the Gardens back and forth across the river every ten minutes or so.

For those spending a bit more time in the area, the *Lone Pine Koala Sanctuary* is one of the most popular attractions. About a forty-five minute bus ride from the center of town (considerably shorter by rental car or taxi), this animal park permits close up visits with kangaroos and koalas, and a chance to observe emus, wombats and even the shy platypus. You can take a very pleasant river cruise to Lone Pine aboard the launch which picks up at the new wharf near the Customs House at the end of Queen street as well as at the old whart at Victoria Bridge fifteen minutes later. This pleasant noon to 5:00 pm trip — or you can go one way by boat and take a bus or taxi back — allows you to see some of Brisbane's more beautiful houses along the river, pass Queensland University of which Brisbanians are particularly proud, see the many bridges over the river, and learn a considerable amount of Brisbanian history from the particularly informative and talkative captain. Be aware that there is a bar but no food served aboard this boat trip; you may want to stop at one of downtown Brisbane's many "take-away" restaurants for sandwiches or a picnic meal which you can eat aboard during the hour or so river trip to Lone Pine. There are snacks available at the koala park if you feel like waiting until mid-afternoon for lunch.

Brisbane of course has many large and small hotels. In earlier days the *Parkroyal* was the favorite, while more recently the new *Sheraton* built atop the rail station is impressive. The view from their fine — if somewhat pricey - - rooftop restaurant is the best in downtown Brisbane. The brand new *Hilton* expects to draw a large portion of visitor interest as well. Even if your program does not call for overnighting in Brisbane, this city can be enjoyed with a brief visit. If your travel schedule allows, you may want to arrange part of a day to enjoy this urbane combination of nineteenth and twentieth centuries.

Marlin Jetty— Cairns

CAIRNS

Cairns likes to call itself the *Gateway to the Great Barrier Reef.* Now that Qantas has inaugurated non-stop service from the West Coast the sobriquet is probably more true than ever. Cairns is the northern end of the east coast Australian rail, road, sea and air transport systems. The city was established purely on possibilities as a port with nothing else to recommend it as site for a city. *Trinity Bay,* around which the city focuses, was named by Captain Cook on Trinity Sunday 1770. The area attracted interest only 100 years later when gold was discovered 200 miles away in 1873 on Palmer River and 1876 on Hodgkinson River. Although no way was ever managed through the mangroves and swamps from Trinity Bay to the gold fields, government officials decided Cairns and Trinity Bay would make a good harbor. The town was officially established in 1876 and was named after the governor of Queensland.

The regional population in the Far North Queensland area serviced by Cairns is about 150,000, growing rapidly during the 1970's and early 1980's, and is considered somewhat maverick in Australian political circles, voting more conservative (that is, Liberal and National Parties rather than Labor) in recent elections than other parts of the country. This may be partly attributable to shifting government attitudes about supporting the sugar cane industry upon which a good part of the state depends.

Cairns' current population is over 50,000, and it is often described as "the mecca for big game fishermen from all over Australia and overseas." Fishing season here is the spring (September through December), and the town's claims to be the best big game fishing place in the world could well be valid. Tuna, barracuda, sailfish, shark, and especially black marlin — the biggest and fiercest of all game fish. Cairns is the black marlin capital of the world. From the Marlin Jetty along Cairns' Esplanade you can watch the marlin being weighed-in. The main swimming beaches are to the north of the city.

Getting from the airport to town is a snap. There are several taxis, and you will also find a friendly limousine service which will take you directly to your hotel or where ever else in town you want to be dropped off for $A3 per person.

Where to Stay

Hotels — or chiefly, motels, in and around the town are abundant. Several of them run courtesy shuttles from the airport, and there is a free reservation telephone board in the arrivals terminal. Evidence of the bustling growth of Cairns is the opening in 1987 of the large *Hilton International* right on the esplanade and in 1988 of the elegant *Park Royal* not far away. Across the way from the Hilton is the modern *Pacific International*. With twelve floors it dominates the local skyline and is located on the Esplanade within sight of the wharf and all of the charter and sight seeing boat services. Both are a block from the main down town area, within easy walking distance of airline offices, banks and stores. Rooms are air conditioned and pleasantly appointed, with color television and international direct dial telephones, and the views of the harbor or the coast are both excellent.

The *Cairns Colonial Club*, opened in 1985 in the Manunda district of Cairns, with 281 rooms is the largest facility in town aside from the Hilton. Although about three miles from downtown, the resort runs an hourly shuttle to the mall as well as free pick-up and delivery at the airport. Rooms are motel style, if a trifle sterile, with color television, direct dial telephones, coffee and tea maker, shower over tub, air conditioning and ceiling fans. Next to their large attractive swimming pool — boulders, a bridge, a waterfall — is a very modestly priced kiosk selling excellent fish and chips and other local fresh fish as well as sandwiches, burgers and the usual poolside snacks. Next to that is the equally fairly priced poolside bar. Both are open until 11:00 p.m. The Homestead Veranda, the resorts main dining area, has an outstanding seafood buffet ($A23) on Friday and Saturday nights with al fresco bistro style dining the remainder of the week. The resort's fancier restaurant, the *Cottage Room*, is in our estimation Cairns' finest. Ask to be seated out on the veranda.

What to do

Naturally the first thing to do after arriving in town is to walk around and get your bearings. If you arrive at lunch time as we did and if you get hungry while walking along the Marlin Jetty and the Esplanade, *Tawny's* offers a wide selection of fresh fish for lunch and dinner and is "fully licensed" (meaning the full range of refreshments are available without having to bring your own.) The baramundi and wrasse were both excellent, and the wine list offered a fine broad selection of Australian wines.

The other leading fresh fish restaurant nearby is the *Waterfront Restaurant* in the *Pacific International Hotel*. Their presentation of Queensland mud crab was outstanding. People in town may recommend that you try *Barnacle Bill's,* also on the Esplanade a block further past the Pacific International; Bill's was popular the   evening we were there, but we concluded it was not likely due to the cuisine.

The town is dotted with small restaurants of a variety of nationalities and offerings — pizza, Chinese, Mexican, Indonesian, local — some licensed to serve alcoholic beverages but most not. Seafood and tropical fruits are restaurant specialties. Local beef raised just down the Queensland coast is highly regarded. There are many long-established Chinese restaurants. The abundance of public bars and bottle shops guarantees that one need not do without suitable refreshment.

If you are interested while you are walking along the wharf, you may want to visit *Reef World* with live   crocodiles on display. If you aren't planning to do any snorkeling or scuba diving in the Reef region, you may be attracted to *Windows On The Reef,* also situated nearby on the waterfront, a floating deck using special effects to give the impression of "diving" 100 feet below surface.

Downtown Cairns bills itself as a shopping stopover with boutiques and chain stores. Actually there is an   abundance of fairly typical tourism shops selling a variety of tee shirts, opal and coral jewelry and fairly typical Australian souvenirs.   If you are interested in purchasing Australian opals, consider buying unset stones to have them mounted in the United States; the Australian jewelers — even in finer locations in Sydney — commonly use 10 carat settings which are not much to American taste. Scattered around Abbott Street and the cross streets are the stores and shops typically found in Australian cities — clothing stores, pharmacies, film and camera stores, small restaurants, bottle shops, and the like, making for a pleasant hour stroll around the town.

There are many day trips available from the jetty at the end of the Esplanade. You can visit Green or Fitzroy Islands, take a day trip to the outer reef (weather permitting), charter a fishing boat for yourself or as part of a group, or just take a half day trip around Trinity Inlet. You may be interested in a guided tour of the *Carlton Brewery* or a visit to the world-famous *flying doctor service* based in Cairns. There are tropical plant and flower nurseries as well as the Botanical Gardens which welcome visitors. To the north of the city are Barron and Freshwater Creek valleys. *Lake Placid* at Barron Gorge is popular as a wild-life sanctuary and is a pleasant picnic spot.

The nearby town of Kuranda can be reached by a trip aboard the restored railroad or half-hour drive from Cairns along fairly good road. The *Kuranda Scenic Rail* — an extremely popular tourist attraction in itself — rises 1000 feet in thirteen miles, passing through fifteen tunnels and a mile of bridges (some over ravines hundreds of feet deep). From Cairns the rail trip is one and a half hours in each direction. Plans are under way for a six-passenger gondola to carry passengers to Kuranda from the Cairns area, through the forests and over *Barron Gorge;* the popularity of this excursion, and a desire not to damage the environment by enlarging the two-lane road, should bring about completion of the world's first jungle tourist gondola by 1990.

Cairns is an excellent place to begin a driving trip of North Queensland and the Barrier Reef coastal areas. There are a few car rental agencies in Cairns, listed under "motor car hire" in the yellow pages or available through your hotel. Do remember to drive LEFT in Australia. Your U.S. or Canadian driver's license is accepted. If you plan to be there at a busy time of year, you had better reserve your car in advance through Hertz, Avis or one of the other international companies which will accept reservations. Incidentally, most rental companies are very cooperative about having you leave your car at the Cairns airport at no additional charge, and drop-off charges generally are   waived or nominal between major points. If you are leaving Cairns via a domestic air carrier, the counter agents will accept your contract and car keys if there is no car drop off office in the particular departure area.

If you do drive to Kuranda, the turnoff from Captain Cook Highway to Kuranda is not clearly marked. We were fortunate that some thoughtful soul had etched "Kuranda" in the dust of the road sign. In case it has rained since we visited, however, turn left at the sign to Mareeba shortly after you have passed the Cairns airport general aviation terminal which is on your right.

Kuranda's main industry today is tourism. Because of its altitude, the town is naturally air conditioned. Just outside of town, or as part of your train ride, you will see *Barron Falls* and *Barron Gorge.* You can take a *Barron River Cruise* aboard the Kuranda Queen departing from the railway station landing daily except Sunday, connecting with all trains. (Sunday hourly departure 10:00 a.m. to 4:00 p.m.)

Army Duck Tours begin at Mountain Groves, which you reach just before entering Kuranda, and take you through rain forest mountains and valleys aboard a six wheel drive amphibian. Tours at 10:00 and 11:30 a.m., and 2:30 p.m. You may enjoy a brief walk through Kuranda which is now two blocks or so of predominantly souvenir and tourist shops. You can lunch in one of their pubs or small restaurants and return to Cairns the way you came.

If you are interested in a longer drive and wish to see some of Australia's interesting interior, consider returning to Cairns with a three hour drive along a loop that takes you across the dairy and farmlands of the region. You can begin to appreciate the huge farms which exist in this land of tremendous open spaces. The crops here include corn and potatoes; tobacco and coffee are grown near Mareeba north of the tableland. There are several tiny towns but they are many miles apart as are residences along the way. As you drive, you will probably notice along the roadside and among the trees puzzling large mounds of dried earthen clay. These are *giant anthills* which, until the advent of new synthetic super-surfaces, provided the material for many of Australia's superb clay tennis courts for which the country enjoyed such fame.

From Cairns your route takes you to Kuranda through *Barron Falls National Park,* then past Kuranda across the Atherton Tableland on the Kennedy Highway toward Mareeba, keeping to the right at the "Y" just before town. Then proceed north to *Mount Molloy* — a former copper mining town now an important cattle and timber center, then bear to the right and proceed northeast on the Julatten Devil Devil Creek Road toward *Mossman* — and important sugar town with its hundred year old working mill — and back to the coast. If you are intending to take this drive, however, remember to get a map of the region from your car rental agency and still be prepared to ask the very friendly locals along the way for directions when the road signs leave you a bit mystified. The road — except where the Queensland government road crews are busy maintaining and improving — is very good for country driving, but do expect occasional flagmen where there is grading going on or a road has been partially washed out during winter flash flooding. As we indicated, however, road signs are not superb.

Right after connecting with the coast highway and starting your southward return to Cairns, you will see   signs on the left to Port Douglas on the coast. This three or four mile detour is well worth a brief visit unless you are very pressed for time. Formerly an important gold rush town, *Port Douglas* is now a small lazy coastal resort and fishing village which is as laid back as you will find. If you haven't had lunch by the time you get there (and it's before 2:00 p.m. when all the local restaurants stop serving) try the *Courthouse Hotel.* You select from the blackboard offering a good choice of grilled dishes, and then walk back to the kitchen to place your order. On your way to or from the kitchen, stop at the pub and order your beer or wine to go with the lunch. There are several pleasant   small hotels and a new *Sheraton* — with a five acre pool - - in Port Douglas for those planning fishing trips or reef excursions based on the coast.

The drive from Port Douglas back to Cairns is about forty-five miles (75 kilometers or so on your Australian odometer) and a very pleasant and picturesque trip along the coast, passing many of Cairns better beaches which are found to the north of the city. You will also pass the new *Ramada Coral Reef* and other resorts at Palm Cove about midway between Port Douglas and Cairns. Should this be your day of departure from Cairns, you will arrive at the airport saving yourself a few miles on the return journey along this same road, and you can drop your rental car there at the airport. If you are interested in seeing Palm Cove and do not wish to drive, the unusual *Hover Mirage* land and water hovercraft inaugurated in late 1987 makes the quick trip from Cairns airport — just across the street from the terminal — to Palm Cove.

TOWNSVILLE

Named for Robert Towns who in 1864 reluctantly decided to approve the site as the rendering works to serve nearby cattle stations, the city originally grew on the strength of the gold rush. Chosen in the late 1950's as the site for a bulk sugar terminal, now new glass and concrete towers dot the city, the most obvious of which is the *sugar shaker* — a cylindrical downtown highrise building housing the *International Hotel,* restaurants, and Australian Airlines (formerly TAA) offices among others. Townsville, Australia's largest tropical city, is the second largest city in Queensland (next to Brisbane) with a current population over 100,000, and if the state ever is split in   two, it is likely this will be capital of Northern Queensland state.

Shopping plazas and malls — particular the new Flinders Mall — give the central business district a very modern look, although there are interesting examples of turn-of-the century commercial architecture standing side by side with the new shops. This international air gateway to the Great Barrier Reef (it will continue to handle flights from Asia, particularly Singapore, New Zealand, and some from Europe and North America, although Cairns was chosen for most of the direct U.S. traffic) is a center of North Queensland commercial development and scientific research. *Captain Cook University*, the *Australian Institute of Marine Science*, and the headquarters of the *Great Barrier Reef Marine Park Authority* are situated here.

The artificial harbor out of Ross Creek is excellent for both large and small boats. From the harbor there is a fine view of Magnetic Island which dominates the skyline five miles across Cleveland Bay. Here Hayle's ferry leaves regularly for the island with ten ferries daily for the forty minute trip. Townsville is the base for day cruises   and air tours to that island as well as for day and overnight trips to the Outer Reef.

The most highly touted accommodations in town are in the new *Sheraton International;* airline and travel reps assume Americans want to stay at the only hotel with a casino. The Sheraton is on the edge of town, however, and many prefer the modern *Townsville International*, dubbed the "sugar shaker" because of its tall circular shape, whose rooms have good views of the city and of Cleveland Bay, balconies, refrigerator, coffee and tea maker, color   TV with in-house movies, and direct dial telephones. In the downtown area there is also *Lowths Hotel*, and near the beach are the *Bessell Lodge International Motel* and the *Townsville Travelodge*, both with good views and facilities. Three new first class hotels are under construction.

A truly unique opportunity exists at *John Brewer Reef* at the *Four Seasons Barrier Reef Floating Hotel* seventy kilometers off Townsville. This floating resort, built in Singapore and floated intact to Australia to be attached to a sunken mooring, has 200 rooms, all with views of the   surrounding reef. Opened at the end of 1987, the resort has three restaurants, two bars, a disco, boutiques, an underwater observation area and live underwater video, and one of the best year-round weather locations on the Barrier Reef. Diving and snorkeling is possible virtually from the hotel's door. Included in the room rates for double rooms without meals ($A364 per night with balcony, $A330 without) and suites ($A450-790) are tennis, swimming pool, gym and sauna, paddle boats, snorkeling equipment and sail boards. Transfers from Townsville are via the Reef Link ($A65 per person round trip) or helicopter ($A200 per person round trip. The resort offers a day trip to nearby reefs ($A60 including lunch) for a maximum of twenty guests and a moonlight champagne cruise ($A50). You can go trawler fishing ($A55) on a working fishing boat, reef fishing — not permitted within the resort area — is available on a day excursion ($A72). (The Four Seasons representative in the United States is at Suite L, 760 West Sixteenth Street, Costa Mesa, California; [800] 654 9153, or in California [800] 922 3559.)

As one would expect in any major urban center, there is plenty of activity in and around Townsville. The *Great Barrier Reef Wonderland* ($A6; $A16 covers movies and museum as well), located on Flinders Street East just a short walk from the downtown Flinders mall, is a unique and impressive aquarium recreation of a barrier reef where coral, plants, fish and other animals — even the sea water — have been relocated from parts of the Great Barrier Reef into two huge display tanks, one for predators and filled with sharks. Visitors walk along beside four inch thick plexiglass viewing windows and through a transparent tube at the bottom of the 125 foot long exhibition looking upward through seventeen feet of water in a million gallon tank to observe a reef ecosystem faithfully recreated with 800 tons of coral reef and 300 tons of sand. Scattered throughout the aquarium are smaller tanks displaying two or three species of fish or crustaceans so they can be observed up close. The exhibition building also houses the first Omnimax Theater in the Southern hemisphere ($A6) with shows every hour, a branch of the Queensland Museum ($A1), and an arcade collection of souvenir, food, dive and travel shops. Lines at the rather inefficiently situated ticket booth were quite long during holidays and weekends, so consider visiting this fascinating marine display early on a weekday if possible.

If you find yourself in Townsville for lunch or dinner, and if you enjoy Chinese cuisine, and if you have been hungering for fresh seafood, consider skipping the several more traditional restaurants in favor of a rare treat. *The Dynasty*, at 228 Flinders East just a block from the mall, labels itself a Chinese seafood restaurant and is probably one of the finest seafood restaurants anywhere in Australia. With three substantial tanks in the entrance with live lobster, giant prawns, and mud crabs, this delightful fully licensed oasis has a menu containing a surprising variety of fresh fish and crustaceans. Prawns taken live from the tank and deep fried, then sauteed in chili sauce, were succulent, tender and sweet — a rare experience. Moreton bay bugs dipped in a light egg batter and coated with a combination of plum and chili sauce were incredible. The chef has an inspired talent for cooking fresh seafood! While not inexpensive for an Australian restaurant, this is a superb dining experience by anyone's standard.

The *Reef Link* ($A70 per person) leaves from the Flinders Street terminal opposite the Greyhound Bus terminal at 9:30 a.m. and returns at 5:00. It carriers up to 144 passengers aboard a 70' catamaran over the 38 miles to the John Brewer Reef at 30 knots in just about 90 minutes. There passengers transfer to floating pontoons which serve as a base from which guests can swim, snorkel and dive. (There is also a helipad.) After a smorgasbord lunch, passengers board the *Yellow Sub*, the semi-submersible which slowly moves across the John Brewer Reef for a forty-five minute ride, during which fish viewed from the sub-sea fisheye glass windows are hand fed by divers alongside. The Reef Link also offers occasional trips to the Palm Islands group, visiting the *Orpheus Island National Park* as well. A separate operation, the *Couger Cat* ($A65 per person), takes forty-five passengers on a fifty foot motor launch to Orpheus Island.

The trip from Townsville to Magnetic is about twenty minutes ($A7.50 round trip) and leaves roughly every hour during daylight via either *Westmark 'Cat'* from the same building which houses the Great Barrier Reef Aquarium or *Hayles Cruises* from a terminal about a block away on Flinders East. The comfortable Westmark boats have a bar and snack counter. Hayles offers a combined ferry ride and day tour of Magnetic Island ($A21.25) including bus and BBQ Grill at one of their two hotels on Magnetic. Hayles also operates the Magnetic vehicle ferry ($A60 round trip for car plus two adults) which departs three times daily — twice daily on weekends — from the opposite side of the Ross Creek estuary from the passenger ferries.

COASTAL TOWNS

The drive along the Bruce Highway takes you through many charming coastal and inland towns. You will find yourself in or near one or more of these small communities if you are accessing barrier reef resort islands from the coast rather than directly by air. For convenience, we have listed the towns alphabetically. If you were to be driving from north to south, however, you will encounter them in the following order: Cooktown and Port Douglas (discussed in our section on Cairns) are north of Cairns; between Cairns and Townsville you pass Mission Beach and Tully, Innisfail, Cardwell, Lucinda and Ingham; from Townsville south you come to Bowen, Airlie Beach and Shute Harbor, Proserpine, Mackay, Rockhampton, Gladstone, and Bundaberg before reaching Brisbane.

Airlie Beach and Shute Harbor

Shute Harbor is the launch departure point for the Whitsunday Group of islands, and Airlie Beach — about five miles away — is the tourist resort, service center and dormitory for visitors to the area. More visitors use Shute Harbor than any other maritime port in Australia, second in traffic only to Circular Cay in Sydney Harbor. Neither boasts a good beach. Whitsunday Field, the home base of Reef World Airline — formerly known as Air Whitsunday, is situated about midway between Shute Harbor and Airlie Beach. Busses and a very occasional taxi connect the two communities as well as linking them with the airport serving Proserpine a few miles away.

Huge catamaran ferries able to carry as many as three hundred passengers call at Shute Harbor serving South Molle and Hamilton Island resorts, and there is a 50-passenger water taxi serving all of the other Whitsunday resorts. Launches take passengers from here to the other Whitsunday Passage islands, and many day trips of the region are based here. Three of the major boat charter companies (*Whitsunday Rent-a-Yacht, Queensland Yacht Charters* and *Australian Bare Boat Charter*) are also situated in Shute Harbor.

This good-sized harbor is very well protected by surrounding hills against almost all of the weather experienced in the region and offers many moorings and ample space for anchorages. It is also a fairly convenient overnight harbor for bareboats and charters cruising the Whitsundays, so there are usually many boats moored in the bay on an average evening. Fresh water is available at the harbor for yachts, and there is a small souvenir and sundries shop as well as an adjoining cafeteria. There are a marina, a hotel and accommodation houses dotted around Shute Harbor.

Airlie Beach (population 2500), five miles north of Shute Harbor — or by road from the north, exit the highway at Proserpine — has grown from a sleepy village a few years ago to a bustling resort town. There are already many motels, lots of camp grounds and *caravans* (trailer parks) as well as several substantial resorts including *The Terraces*, and *Whitsunday Village. Wanderers Paradise*, Melanesian family-style unitswith refrigerator, stove, crockery, laundry facilities, nightly entertainment, swimming pools, and tennis courts, was formerly owned by Australian Airlines which recently sold the resort. However, the best hotel in town is probably the *Coral Sea Resort* with similar facilities. Very nice apartments are also available for weekly or monthly rental.

There is a post office, many souvenir and T-shirt shops, and the news agency (mid-way along the town's main street on the west side) with an excellent selection of books on Australia, yachting, fishing, as well as general reading material. There are Australian Airlines and Ansett reservations office and several travel and sightseeing booking agencies, physicians' offices, two firms of solicitors (lawyers, that is, one of which you will need should you wish to acquire or convey property here), a large super market, yacht sales and rental offices, and Avis and Budget car rental agencies, among other businesses.

For a town of this size, Airlie Beach has an exceptional supply of good restaurants. *Romeo's,* set back from the east side of the street between a travel agency and a hair salon, is an outstanding Italian restaurant which could hold its own, indeed excel, in almost any American city. The restaurant is right on the beach, and there is seating on the beach veranda, inside or in a pleasant front courtyard. Service was very attentive, and the owner personally supervises both the open kitchen and the dining room.

Romeo's fresh pasta was absolutely superb; the fresh fish even more outstanding, particularly the succulent barbecued Moreton Bay bugs (those miniature lobsters from South Queensland, served about six to a portion, covered with garlic butter). Adjoining the restaurant is a gourmet take-out deli. Romeo himself is a transplanted Melbournean who refused all our blandishments and cajolery to get him to relocate in the United States.

In minds of many equal to Romeo's is *Seagull's Bistro* in Cannonvale just to the north of Airlie Beach. This BYO — that is, not licensed to serve alcohol — seafood restaurant is extremely innovative and inexpensive. Rolf and Margaret are the owners: he the chef and she in charge of the dining room.

Bowen

Midway between Townsville and Mackay, **Bowen** (population 8000) is a small colonial town with pretty beaches on three sides backed by hills on the fourth. The district is a veritable garden with fruit, cane, vegetables and widely regarded mangoes grown in the region. One ex-local familiar with the region tells us the town "used to be called blowin' but it got the 'l blowed out of it."

Bundaberg

Bundaberg is the access point for Lady Elliot Island and is also a take-off point from which many day cruises to the reef, including Lady Musgrave Island, depart. It is known as the *rum-making capitol* of Queensland, with its annual production of half a million gallons of Bundaberg rum distributed all across Australia. *Buss Park,* in the middle of town on the Burnett River, has a good view of the trawlers which base here. The city is surrounded by cane fields and sugar refineries. *Mon Repos beach* a few miles to the east is a large turtle nesting ground from late November through March where visitors can watch loggerhead, flatback and green turtles lay their eggs in the sand.

Cardwell

West of Rockingham Bay, protected by the heights of Hinchinbrook Island, **Cardwell** is a center of a major national park area and is near Australia's *bananaland.* Located on Bruce Highway about mid-way between Townsville and Cairns, it is a very small resort town which fills up during holidays with people interested in boating and fishing. The town has a small private reptile park, a golf course and bowling green, a swimming pool and tennis courts. Short excursions to nearby national parks are easily arranged.

There is no anchorage; small boats and various charter cruises share the single concrete wharf. Here you can rent house boats, power boats and yachts for plying the Hinchinbrook Channel and may also take sailing lessons if you wish. The *Reef Venture II* leaves for day trips — and to carry resort visitors — for the half hour trip across the channel to Hinchinbrook Island ($A26 per person round trip) daily except Monday at 9:00 and returns from the island at 4:30. Visitors may disembark either at the resort's jetty or at *Macushla Bay* where they can picnic or hike through the rain forrest — about an hour and a half walk — to Cape Richards where the resort is situated.

Cooktown

This is the most northern center of population on the eastern coast, and it is about as far as you can go by road without special equipment. Captain Cook's ship, the *Endeavor,* found shelter here in 1770; there is a monument marker where the ship was beached. About this near-ghost town full of character (but only 920 people), the Australian Tourist Commission says, "Some 80 years ago gold brought overnight prosperity to Cooktown. The ghosts of times past are the few remaining great solid banks which face a main street of gentle grass and lush trees." This was the first place a kangaroo was ever seen by a European — Cook's party.

During the Palmer River gold rush 100 years later Cooktown became the center of Australia's northern gold boom. The population swelled to 5000 making it Queensland's second largest city at the time. There were some sixty- five hotels in town. When the rush petered out, Cooktown's boom economy collapsed. You can still visit many of the old buildings which have survived the ravages of cyclones over the years. There is also the *James Cook Historical Museum* housed in the old Convent of St. Mary and the surrounding *Joseph Banks Gardens,* named for Cook's botanist. Other popular points are the *Cooktown Sea Museum,* the *Cemetery* where many of the 20,000 Chinese prospectors who came to work the goldfields are buried, and *Grassy Hill* where Cook climbed to search the sea for a passage to the north.

Gladstone

Aside from being the departure point for Heron Island, **Gladstone** (population 22,000) is an industrial town 350 miles north of Brisbane which boasts the world's largest aluminum refinery, processing almost three million tons a year. A 1 1/2 hour catamaran trip takes visitors to nearby Mast Head Island. There is a small six-unit resort ($A75 per person per day full board) on Quoin Island three miles from the city.

Ingham

With a diverse ethnic population including residents of Italian, Basque, Spanish and Flemish extraction, **Ingham** (population 14,000) is a flourishing sugar cane city adjacent to the Hinchinbrook Channel with two mills. *Victoria Sugar Mill* conducts guided tours throughout the season. It is here that both the terrain, vegetation and weather transition from the tropical north coast of Queensland to the sub- tropical center coast. Because of this transitional location Ingham boasts the highest annual rainfall in Australia; Tully to the north also boasts the highest annual rainfall— leading to a friendly competition yearly to see which town records the most precipitation.

Innisfail

Thought by some to be the prettiest town on the coast and (because of its position next to the mountains), **Innisfail** (population 8000) is just over fifty miles south of Cairns. One of the wettest towns on the continent, it is surrounded by heavy tropical growth because of the Johnstone and South

Innisfail

Johnstone Rivers on its doorsteps. On one side of the river the tropical rainforest comes right down to the edge, while on the opposite bank there are pleasant grassy picnic areas.

Innisfail, about four miles from the coast, was a center for *blackbirding,* the nineteenth century trade in Pacific islands slaves for cane work in the lush fields surrounding the town. After the Palmer River gold supply dwindled, many Chinese drifted to Innisfail; later many   Italian laborers were brought in. During World War II many of the Italians were interned, but since then the town has become a harmonious multi-ethnic community.

Five miles south of town you will find Mourilyan with Queensland's only sugar museum as well as a roadside pub and cafe. At the harbor you can watch sugar loaded onto huge ships at the terminal. Inland from Innisfail is the Nerada Tea Plantation, the only one in Australia, where you can take a tour and enjoy the local tea.

Lucinda

On Hinchinbrook Channel, **Lucinda** (population 600) is primarily a facility for large ships to load cane sugar   and molasses. The bulk sugar wharf is probably the longest of its type in the world, an amazing 3-mile long slender jetty completed in 1979 permitting ships to load and unload without having to enter the Hinchinbrook Channel.

Mackay

A business and tourist city surrounded by tropical palms and parks, **Mackay** (population 40,000) is the sugarcane capitol of Australia. Established in 1860 it now produces one third of Australia's sugar. Situated 600 miles north of Brisbane on the Pioneer River, its large artificial harbor hosts the *world's largest sugar terminal,* able to store 700,000 tons, and also a large open-cut coal handling complex. In addition to being a departure point for island resorts and the outer reef, attractions in this tropical city include the *Botanic Gardens, Mt. Bassett* and *Mt. Oscar* both with great city views, guided tours of the sugar terminal, walking tracks and excellent views in *Fungella National Park,* tropical rainforest and attractive   beaches. There are launch and air tours to coral reefs and offshore islands. Dolphin Heads is a new beachfront resort town ten minutes north of Mackay.

Mission Beach and Tully

Named because of the presence of an Aboriginal Mission between 1914 and 1918, Mission Beach (population 650) is the main local access point to Dunk and Bedarra Islands. Located 140 miles north of Townsville and 85 miles south of Cairns, locals refer to this as the *real tropics.* Separated from the Bruce Highway by several miles of rain forest — it is about a fifteen mile detour to visit Mission Beach, this is one of the only areas of lowland rain forest left in the tropics and is the only surviving remnant at sea level. Turning east from the highway at Tully from the south or El Arish to the north, you drive through beautiful farmlands and tropical woods known as complex mesophyl lowland vineforest. You can see ferns, vines, orchids, and wild ginger. The abundant red volcanic soil in the region accounts for some of the largest bananas grown in Australia on the plantations you will pass.

The forest is inhabited by cassowary (a large flightless bird slightly smaller than the emu or the ostrich), scrubfowl, parrots, wallaby and numerous varieties of large tropical butterflies. We were cautioned not to feed the cassowaries, as there has been an unfortunate increase in the number of road deaths of these rare birds due to their associating food with cars and venturing onto the roads. In addition to bananas, there are pineapple and paw paw (papaya) plantations and a Sunday morning market at Wongaling Corner. Mission Beach North has an amazingly beautiful long expanse of sandy beach with the lush tropical forest coming right down to the shore. Look for mangoes, papaya, banana, bougainvillaea and palm.

The *Mission Beach Resort* is situated south of the tiny town in the rain forest close to the beach. It features air conditioned rooms with radio, color television, telephones, tea and coffee maker. The large pleasant motel style rooms are organized in clumps with a central swimming pool — divided into children's pool, deep pool and (unheated) spa — and gas barbecue in each area. The resort has a restaurant and a tavern. There are well marked walking tracks through the forest. There is tennis, a pitch and putt course, and a gym with a squash court and a sauna. Next to the resort is a small shopping center with a bottle shop, market, souvenir and clothing shops and a small Chinese restaurant.

In town is the new *Castaways Beach Resort* with catamarans, water skiing, paddle skis, tennis, swimming, and wind surfing. Through the resorts you can arrange several excursions. There is a cassowary tour combined with a banana safari ($A14), a day sail on the 52' *Neptunius* to Dunk Island and the Family Island group ($A50 including lunch), a reef fishing excursion ($A70), flightseeing from Tully ($A49) or Dunk ($A45) in a special plexiglass nose aircraft. Aside from several launch and taxi services available from the town, *Island Coast Air Services* provides reef and inland excursions. From both Mission Beach South and the Clump Point Jetty at the north edge of town, there are water taxis to Dunk Island. *Friendship Cruises* operates day tours from Clump Point to Beaver Cay on the Great Barrier Reef ($A44; bring your own lunch) and day trips to Dunk Island ($A12). The *M.V. Quick Cat* offers similar trips to Dunk ($A14 round trip) and Beaver Cay ($A66 including lunch and a stopover on Dunk).

About twenty miles inland from the coast, nearby Tully is another center of the sugar growing district, producing one million tons of cane per year. It is also   known for bananas and other tropical fruits as well as for cattle ranching. King Ranch, the well known American concern, has developed area covering approximately 50,000 acres to the west. With 170 inches of rain yearly, Tully vies with Ingham for the claim to the highest average annual rainfall of any town in Australia. The *Raft & Rainforest Co.* offers white water rafting trips daily on the Tully ($A60) and Barron ($A30) Rivers and two day trips on the North Johnstone; they will even pick you up in Cairns or Townsville.

Proserpine

Proserpine (population around 6000) is noted for its   sugar mill, and guided tours are available during the crush season. To the west a new dam has been constructed allowing a large fresh water recreation area.

Rockhampton

Rockhampton (population 50,000) is a provincial city on the banks of the Fitzroy River which can be brown and muddy and not terribly attractive. The town looks much   like a small U.S. town circa 1945. This area is famous for beef cattle and is also a sugar cane center. Quay Street in the city, one block from the main downtown shopping street, is intact from its 19th century beginnings, but little has been done to make the street or the town particularly attractive to tourists. *Rocky* is the access point for Great Keppel Island and is not really worth a special visit; if you have time between planes or whatever, try the *Heritage Tavern* on Quay Street for an ample, inexpensive, and quite pleasant lunch.

on Hayman Island

More
Interesting
Things

In this chapter we pass along information about a few additional ideas for vacation activities, a word about departure formalities, and some potential useful sources of additional information.

Sightsailing and Flightseeing

Sailing or flying to the Outer Barrier Reef or around groups of islands is an easy and reasonably economical way   of exploring areas of the Great Barrier Reef and its cays, atolls and islands. The *M.V. Quicksilver*, a high speed catamaran with bar, sun deck, freshwater shower and swimming platform and operated by the same people who run the day trip to the Low Islets, leaves Port Douglas wharf daily at 10:00 a.m. for three and a half hours at Agincourt Reef on the Outer Barrier Reef ($A70, drinks extra; $A78 includes round trip bus connection from Cairns). There in the Coral Sea you can swim, snorkel, explore via semi-submersible subs, view the reef from their underwater observatory, and scuba dive (they will rent you equipment if you hold a certificate from a recognized dive organization). The cruise includes smorgasbord lunch including fresh prawns, a video film about the Great Barrier Reef and free use of equipment (except scuba gear and underwater cameras which must be rented). The *Quicksilver* returns to Port Douglas at 4:30 p.m.

Sundance Cooktown Cruises ($A79 from Cairns, including lunch) departs Port Douglas at 9:15 Tuesday through Sunday for a trip to Cooktown with stops at islands along the way. The *M.V. Sunbird* runs from Cairns to Townsville, passing uninhabited and resort islands along the way. There are day charters for game and marlin fishing from Cairns as well as several other island visit cruises. The reservations office is situated right on the wharf on the Esplanade. There are also numerous extended cruises — up to a 14 day cruise aboard *M.V. Auriga Bay* to Thursday Island at the northeast tip of Australia — which can be booked from Cairns. Similarly from Townsville there are numerous one- and multi-day cruises to nearby islands and to the Outer Reef.

From *Mackay Roylen Cruises* operates five-day cruises aboard the 114' *M.V. Roylen Endeavor* carrying 45 passengers in air conditioned cabins throughout the year ($A645 per person, double bed suite, meals included; $A557, cabins with private baths; $466, cabins with shared facilities). These trips call at the Great Barrier Reef (weather permitting), the Whitsunday Islands and Brampton Island. A similar eight-day cruise from Mackay is operated aboard the 112' vessel *Elizabeth E II* ($A942, meals included).

Reef World Airways (formerly Air Whitsunday), P.O. Box 166, Airlie Beach, Qld. 4802; telephone: [79] 469 133, offers several *Reef Adventures*. There are many   brief sightseeing flights ($A20-75, depending upon length) over the Outer Reef. On Wednesdays they will fly you to the 112' *T.S.M.V. Reef Encounter Sandra,* moored at the Outer Reef for a full day at Hardy Reef ($A115 inclusive, without scuba gear), departing Whitsunday Field at 8:00 a.m. The day is spent reef walking, snorkeling, coral viewing on a glass bottomed boat, scuba diving (if you are qualified), or fishing, with lunch included. For longer stays, the *Reef Encounter,* with crew of 9 including PADI dive instructor and marine biologist, has twin cabin accommodations for a maximum of 25 guests. ($A490, 7 days, inclusive except scuba; $A440 5 days; $A245 two days; $A165 Saturday a.m. to Sunday p.m.; $158 overnight.) In addition, Reef World offers scuba diving packages at the Reef Encounter from 2 days ($A305) to 7 days ($640), with an introductory shallow water training and single-dive "resort course" ($A45) and additional instructed dives ($A30 first dive, $A20 second dive, including all gear and an instructor buddy). All necessary scuba gear can be rented, including regulators and even (by arrangement 24 hours prior to the flight) underwater Nikonos cameras and strobes.

For their *piece de resistance* Reef World offers a *Great Barrier Reef Flying Boat Cruise* ($A1870 per person, twin accommodations, inclusive) which departs either Cairns or Brisbane and includes visits to Dunk, Hinchinbrook and Orpheus Islands, Brewer Reef and the Yellow Sub, Hardy Lagoon, the Reef Encounter, Great Keppel Island, Lady Musgrave Island and Fraser Island. This one excursion,   operated in the tradition of Flying Boat style, incorporates a broad cross-section of Great Barrier Reef activities and some of its finest attractions.

Further information regarding Reef World Airlines may also be obtained through SO/PAC, 1448 15th Street, Suite 105, Santa Monica, California 90404; telephone [213] 393-8262 or [800] 472-5015, or Maritime World, 2618 Newport Blvd., Newport Beach, California 92663; telephone [714] 675-2250, reservations collect.

Cairns

Bareboat Charters in the Whitsundays

An increasingly popular way to see the Whitsunday Group of islands is by *chartering a yacht or motor cruiser* from one of the many charter companies operating on the   coast or Hamilton Island. Currently there are accommodations for over four hundred people available on charter boats in this one region, and many people are using this method to see several resort and uninhabited islands without restricting   themselves to a single hotel. Charters are possible with or without crew and on boats of a wide variety of sizes and shapes.

Australian Bareboat Charters P.O. Box 115, Airlie Beach, Qld. 4802; telephone [79] 469-381) includes in its fleet yachts from 25' to 47' and 36' motor cruisers.   They also book the 75' crewed Pegasus which accommodates 8 very comfortably. *Whitsunday Rent-a-Yacht* (Shute Harbour, 4802, Qld; telephone [79] 469 232) has yachts ranging from 22' to 60' and 34' motor cruisers. *Mandalay Sailing* (P.O. Box 218, Airlie Beach, Qld. 4802; telephone [79] 466 298), which operates its own marina outside of Airlie Beach, rents yachts from 25' to 50' and 30' and 34' motor cruisers. Hamilton Island also has charter yacht services. Weekly bare boat rates (that is, without crew or provisions) run from $A750-2500 depending upon length and capacity, with some boats having four berths and others six or eight. Provisions will run $A15-20 per day per person additional. Crew is $A70-100 extra per crew member.

Boats are usually fully equipped with dinghies and outboards, bed linens, kitchen equipment, short wave radio, and fishing gear. All of the charter operators will be pleased to send you current brochures with prices and schematic drawings of the boats showing facilities and accommodations. One bit of advice: unless you really enjoy tightly compacted crowds, discount the charterer's estimate of comfortable accommodations by 25-50% in deciding how many to include in your group, particularly if you are planning more than a few days aboard.

Additional information regarding charters may be obtained from *Yachting World Yacht Charters*, 680 Beach Street, Suite 498, San Francisco, California 94109; telephone [415] 928-4480 or [800] 227-5436, or SO/PAC, 1448 15th Street, Suite 105, Santa Monica, California 90404; telephone [213] 393-8262 or [800] 472-5015

Departure formalities

Australia exacts a departure tax for every person 12 years of age and over of $A20 before leaving Australia, paid at special windows at international airports. A stamp indicating that the tax has been paid is affixed to your plane tickets, so you should allow time for taking care of this before you check in for your flight. Formerly stamps could be purchased in Australian currency only, but now the tax stamp offices in Sydney and Melbourne will accept all major credit cards. Cairns is still cash only, so keep some spare. (We felt the $A20 tax was charged basically to support all the people they hire to check your papers on exiting the country, a formality we had not encountered in such exacting detail in many a year.)

More Information

There are several excellent sources of information fairly easily available to American tourists which will give you current prices, resort sizes, telephone numbers and the like. The first thing you probably should do when you are ready to plan your trip is to contact the Australian Tourist Commission, 2121 Avenue of the Stars, Los Angeles, CA 90067; tel: (213) 552-1988, or Suite 2908, 1270 Avenue of the Americas, New York, NY 10020; tel: (212) 687-6300; telex 23 640 747. Ask them to send you the latest editions of their publication Australia: The Aussie Holiday Book and as well as any information they may be able to send regarding islands in which you are interested.

The international air carriers can provide you with limited information about Great Barrier Reef vacations. Both of Australia's domestic carriers maintain offices in North America, and reservations and travel arrangements can be made through them.

Hinchinbrook Island

Ansett Airlines of Australia
9841 Airport Boulevard
Suite 418
Los Angeles, California 90045

[213] 642-7487

[800] 626-7388 in California

[800] 426-7388 outside of California

Australian Airlines
Nationwide information: [800] 922-5122

230 Park Avenue, Suite 921
New York, New York 10169
Information: [212] 986-3772

510 West Sixth Street, Suite 517
Los Angeles, California 90014
Information and reservations: [213] 626-2352

225 North Michigan Avenue, Suite 930
Chicago, Illinois 60601
Information: [312] 565-0803

P.O. Box 2517
Kirkland, Washington 98083
Sales office: [206] 822-0730

For further information regarding any of the island resorts and particularly as to making reservations for any that do not have U.S. booking agents, contact the Queensland Tourist and Travel Corp., 611 No. Larchmont, Los Angeles, California 90004; telephone [213] 465-8418; telex 25 9103214333.

There are seven Australian consular offices in the United States and three in Canada:

Australian Consulate-General
636 Fifth Avenue
New York NY 10111
[212] 245-4000

Australian Consulate-General
Suite 2930, Quaker Tower
321 North Clark Street
Chicago IL 60610
[312] 645-9444

Australian Consulate-General
611 North Larchmont Boulevard
Los Angeles CA 90046
[213] 380-8098, 3801455, or 380-6337

Australian Embassy
1601 Massachusetts Avenue NW
Washington DC 20036-2273
[202] 797-3222

Australian Consulate-General
1990 Post Oak Blvd., Suite 800
Houston TX 77056-9998
[713] 629-9140 or 629-9138

Australian Consulate Penthouse Suite
1000 Bishop Street
Honolulu HI 96813-4299
[808] 524-5050

Australian High Commission
The National Building
13th Floor 130 Slater Street
Ottawa ONT K1P5H6
[613] 236-0841

Australian Consulate-General
P.O. Box 12519
Oceanic Plaza Suite 800
1066 West Hastings Street
Vancouver BC V6E3X1
[604] 684-1177

Australian Consulate-General
Commerce Court North
Suite 2200
King & Bay Streets
Commerce Court Postal Station Box 69
Toronto ONT M5L1B9
[406] 367-0783

Share the Reef

Without doubt Australia's Great Barrier Reef offers a unique variety of tropical vacation experiences. From intimate to large, low to mountainous, informal to elegant, this collection of resorts has it all. This exciting menu is offered on a series of refreshingly uncrowded islands where a thousand people (as on Hamilton) is a veritable metropolis, while a guest population of sixty or less (perhaps Lizard, Orpheus or Hinchinbrook are more your cup of tea) is not at all out of the ordinary. Set all this down in one of the world's truly spectacular natural structures and you have the makings for many memorable journeys.

Day by day the area is becoming more popular. Australians are discovering their national treasure, and Americans are not far behind, particularly while the U.S. dollar remains strong against Australia's dollar. Resorts are expanding (yet blessedly modestly by U.S. standards), although the government is committed to the proposition that remaining uninhabited islands will stay undeveloped.

But change here is, as everywhere, inevitable. During the intervals between our visits, the major regional airline was acquired by the government owned national carrier, a new resort's central complex burned to the ground and was rebuilt within six months with no trace of the disaster, another resort announced a complete cessation of operations for nine months during major remodeling — a hiatus which in fact stretched an additional year before the resort reopened, another old line family resort sold to a national airline, two resorts doubled their capacity (from thirty to a mere sixty guests on an entire island), and another completed plans to move the resort from one side of the tiny island to the other.

Fortunately here change is almost always modest and moderate. With but one resort facility to most of these islands, growth still means you will always be able to find a private spot on a quiet beach for a lovely picnic, sail in uncrowded waters or snorkel in beautiful tropical lagoons, finding privacy or activity as you desire.

By the time you visit the area, perhaps the $A3 billion Aqualung, a giant two story clear acrylic entertainment center with restaurants, three cocktail bars, coffee lounges and walkways a hundred feet below the sea off Cairns, will be completed. Maybe Hamilton's projected Mediterranean resort will be opened. Elsewhere there undoubtedly will be more and more submersibles (these remarkable new power barges that cruise

Arne and Ruth Werchick

around on the surface of the lagoons with their huge under-water windows) visiting the reef, more flights to and around the area, more boats for hire, more hotel rooms, all the while preserving vast open spaces, uncrowded beaches, dense forests, friendly resorts. There will undoubtedly be more air service from North America to Cairns and Brisbane.

We hope that your travels to this remarkable region are as filled with pleasure as ours have been. We would be indebted to those of you who could find the time to share your Great Barrier Reef experiences with us. A postcard from your favorite island, a note to keep us abreast of changes, even a memo setting right anything you think   needs correcting will be much appreciated. Send your comments to us

Arne and Ruth Werchick

c/o Wide World Publishing/Tetra
P.O. Box 476
San Carlos, California 94070

to let us know what's happening in our favorite corner of the world. And give a scrap of your breakfast fruit to a friendly wallaby or a piece of bread to a passing parrot fish for us.

Other Travel Books by
Wide World Publishing/Tetra

THE YUCATAN
A Guide to the Land of Maya Mysteries
by Antoinette May
$9.95

HIGH CITIES OF THE ANDES
by Celia Wakefield
$9.95

EXPLORING POINT REYES
A Guide to Point Reyes National Seashore
by Phil Arnot & Elvira Monroe
$5.95

POINT REYES
Secret Places & Magic Moments
by Phil Arnot
$9.95

BIG SUR
"The Coast Wild and Lonely"
by Rosalind Sharpe Wall
$9.95

HAWAII—Island Paradise
*A collection of impressions about Hawaii
by famous travelers.*
—Illustrated—

Other Travel Related Books

Hawaii—Cooking with Aloha	$7.95
Greek Cooking for Everyone	$7.95
The English Rose Cookbook	$9.95